HOW ON EARTH?

A STORY OF ORDINARY PEOPLE
AND AN EXTRAORDINARY GOD

HELEN MEKIE WITH GRACE LONGMIRE

Text © 2018 Helen Mekie

Email: helenmekie@gmail.com

First edition 2018

Text design by Kim Hough

Cover design by Fiona Ruttle

ISBN 13: 978-1726259040

ISBN 10: 1726259048

CONTENTS

PREFACE

I was born, the second of twins, during an air raid during World War II, and so my first impressions must have been of noise, danger and darkness. I grew up in a home that seemed a stranger to happiness and of course I was miserable and realized I had to find an answer to survive. I thought God was my only hope, bought a Bible, read it from cover to cover and found as I finished that I had fallen in love with the God who goes to every length to reach people even as lost as I was.

Of course this meant that I wanted to do whatever He had for me, and so the rest of my life has been about trying to become more as He wants me to be, and to go wherever He says, and try and do whatever He asks.

Unfortunately this did not solve all my problems but at least pointed me in the right direction. I made it through school, was good at games and not much else.

On leaving school I went to Bedford College to learn how to teach sport, and then did so at a school in Cardiff.

After teaching for 2 years I trained as a nurse and became a sister at the Middlesex Hospital running an oncology ward.

I was miserable, and realized that I had to find an answer to survive.

Meeting Grace Longmire changed everything for me, and again and again I have been asked to write a book telling our stories. I didn't want to write a biography, but rather to share the stories, with just enough of us in them to make sense. Because stories, particularly when they are personal and told by perfectly ordinary and unlikely individuals, encourage all of us.

You will find bits of a whole lot of other people's stories in here too. Each one has their own place and great value, and has added hugely to the richness of what has been lifetimes of being involved in what is going on.

Rather than list them or put in just a few at the cost of all, please accept that every thing you did is honoured and remembered, particularly by the individuals involved.

Having said that, I would like to mention those who made this book possible:

Fiona and family who, confronted with the request to do a cover for the book, obliged with everything they had, even though it was outside their normal focus.

Kim, who has been the kindest and most helpful of editors, and who also did the DTP for this book.

Jane, who has been there all along, providing that practical grace and wisdom which is why we have got this far.

Finally, this is the result.

IT WASN'T SUPPOSED
TO BE LIKE THIS ...

We were somewhere in central Asia on our way to help the Hippies. Only we weren't. Instead we had been stopped, firstly by a large log across the road, and then by a crowd of men in long robes, who rapidly surrounded us as we reluctantly skidded to a halt.

They indicated we should get out. Instead, somewhat futilely, we locked the doors. Their response was to surround the car, and pick it up. I have never felt more helpless. Or, more angry. I didn't mind dying, after all we all die sometime, and I knew Afghanistan wasn't thought to be the safest destination in the world, but I minded terribly being killed before we even got there.

As the car rose to waist height I said to Grace "What do you suggest?" "Try praying", she answered, and clearly followed her own advice. By then the men had lifted the car to shoulder height and we were in danger of being tossed upside down. I took up her suggestion and joined Grace in flat out prayer. The strangest, or most wonderful thing happened. All the men let go of our vehicle at the same moment as though it had become too hot to handle. We landed back on the road with considerable impact. When the dust settled they were in a large circle staring at us. The log was gone.

One of the men came forward and spoke to Grace. "What is he saying," I asked. (In all this I had discovered that one of her many unknown-to-me abilities was that she spoke rudimentary Arabic) She smiled as she answered that they were asking us to leave. We did so, as quickly as we could. It took us a long time however to stop shaking, and I still say "Thank You" every time I remember the incident and the terror I felt.

Of course, the question must be what on earth were we doing in central Asia anyway. The answer is that it was the next stage in the journey we were making through our lives. For Grace it was very much going on with more of the same, for me a radical and unexpected change. Let me start at the beginning.

GRACE'S STORY

Grace Longmire grew up in Kendal in the Lake District of England. It is a beautiful old town with lots of ancient houses, a castle, the home of K Shoes – one of the big shoe making companies of England, and not forgetting Kendal Mint Cake, beloved of climbers attempting Mount Everest,

She was the second child in the family born less than a year after her sister, and to a mother who was an asthmatic and often ill (this was before the days of the national health, and medical care was expensive). Her sailor father was mostly away at sea, and so both she and her sister had to learn to cope for themselves quite early She took herself off to school at the age of two, and attacked life with all she had. Her parents were committed Christians, and she acquired a deep and personal faith while still at junior school. This, in her words, helped her cope with the pressures at home when her mother was ill.

When she left school Grace went to college, to train to be a teacher.

Being Grace, she was involved in everything, particularly sport at which she was very good. So good in fact, that the possibility of her playing hockey for England at some future date was very real. She also belonged to a Christian group that met every month.

She was fairly sure where her future lay; getting a good teaching job, buying a car, travelling, eventually getting her own house, and of course playing hockey. So when the Christian group seemed to have an undue number of speakers who talked about the mission field, and giving the rest of one's life to some foreign country, normally the Far East, she rather wanted to avoid those.

But that particular month she reckoned, if the title was anything to go by, she was safe. It was a slide show on Africa. It was interesting, and she was enjoying it when a deep conviction overtook her. She knew, with that certainty that brooks no argument, that God wanted her to go with Him and for Him to Africa. She knew it. It was not welcome news. That night she spent a very long time talking to God. Finally she gave Him all the plans she had made and accepted His. She would qualify, spend two years teaching, go to Bible College, and then wherever God sent her in Africa.

She has never regretted it. She spent six years in Eritrea and more than forty years in South Africa.

She also bought a car, did more travelling than she dreamed of, and owns her own home.

As for the hockey, she picked up an injury while playing in the English hockey trials which never really healed and prevented top class competition from then on.

God heard the desires of her heart and gave them to her

THE SLOG REPLACED

After training to be a teacher and then going to Bible College, Grace went to Eritrea to teach in a mission school in a Muslim area. She was there for five years learning the local languages, and giving further training to the local teachers who taught the girls. It was quite unusual in those days that there was a school for girls, and the teachers welcomed the chance to increase their skills and qualifications.

On her way back to England for a 6-months stint, which was supposed to be some rest with some speaking engagements and turned out to be lots of speaking and some rest, she looked back at her time in the school. She had worked hard, learned the languages surprisingly well, done everything she had been asked to do, and seen some results. She should have felt good. But she very definitely did not. In her own words "It was such a slog". She didn't want to go back to more of the same. She loved the work, and she loved the people. But, inescapably, it was dissatisfying. And clearly that is not Good News. Perhaps others found it good enough. For Grace it was not.

So, she was looking for and needing something that would bring about essential change. As she spoke at all the meetings that had been arranged for her, met all the people who wanted to talk to her, and tried to get some sort of rest and refreshment in the small intervals allowed in the schedule, her constant prayer was for a major change to happen. Without it, there was no going back.

As she went from group to group scattered all over the UK, she began to notice some individuals who seem to have 'something indefinable' that she knew she wanted. What it was she didn't know, but she did know she wanted it. She began to look for 'it', and found whatever 'it' was all over the place. So she started to ask those who had this indefinable thing what it was. "The Holy Spirit" was the answer she was given each time. Perhaps this was the answer to the problem of it all being 'such a slog.'

Of course she had known Him, the Holy Spirit, before, as she had known the Father and Jesus. But the part of the church she had grown up in believed that the acts of the Spirit found in the New Testament were only for that time. A sort of 'get the church going, until it can manage by itself,' understanding. They did not, on the whole, expect the Holy Spirit to work in power in ordinary folk in the present time. So, while believing very much in Him with her head, as it were, the thought of Him empowering her or giving her the gift of healing or working of miracles and so on, was outside her box.

But Grace was desperate, and if the Holy Spirit was touching others why not her? She was more than ready to accept anything from Him that she had been missing out on. She prayed, and He came in a new way, and Grace knew it. Without any doubt. What happened that day was only the start of a significant change. She said little of it to those around her, and rather focused on getting used to the new dimension she was experiencing.

She said nothing of what had happened on her return (yes, she went back assured that it would not be the same slog), but they noticed. Some weeks after her return to the school in Eritrea where she was teaching, she was going through the passage in John's gospel where Jesus talks of having come that His followers would have life and have it to the full. In Tigrinya, the local language of the people, that is translated as *having life, and that which is extra life.* "That is it!" one of the teachers exclaimed, "When you were here before you had life. Then you went away. When you came back you had that which is extra life. What happened? We have seen the difference, and we all want what you have found."

They had seen that the 'slog' had been replaced by a new power, ability and freshness, and it had made them hungry, for they too found it a slog. Grace shared with them what had happened to her, and they asked for and received the same experience of the Holy Spirit coming in a new way, and giving them a power and freedom that did indeed make a difference. It was the beginning of a very different, wonderful time in the area when many who were Christians found a new lease of life and many who were not yet Christians found the giver of the extra and were transformed as a result.

It was a glorious time for many, and crossed cultural and religious barriers as individuals were blessed. This was a time of rare change and freedom, and many from the community wanted to be part of it. Not just because of healings and miracles, but also the peace and personal help they found. Here are some of her stories.

RATS

Grace looked out of the window of the school where she was teaching in Eritrea and saw an enormous rat crossing the yard. She thought that they need to get rid of it as it could bite one of the children. So she went down and spoke to Fanuel, the caretaker. They found the rat hole it had disappeared into and Fanuel's face lit up. "Oh, that's easy he said, I will put down some rat poison." "No, you will not," said the headmistress, who had come into the discussion. "One of the children might eat it and die." She had no alternative suggestions, and they parted with the problem of the rat unresolved.

Grace went back to her room and prayed. She had no liking for rats, and could see that one rat could well become several, and getting bitten was also a problem. "Please God, we are not allowed to put down rat poison, and I don't know what we can do, please would you deal with the rat. Please."

Two days later she saw a cat jump onto the high wall that surrounded the school compound. She had not seen cats at the school before, and she caught her breath in anticipation. Could this be God's answer to her prayer? She watched as it sat there, and then, finally, jumped down into the compound, went into the hole and disappeared. Over the next hour the cat reappeared with a dead rat, which it left for display in the courtyard, and then twice reappeared with other dead rats. By now Grace's excitement had alerted the headmistress to the presence of the cat. When three rats were stretched out, clearly dead, the cat sat down cleaned itself, and then jumped back on the wall and disappeared.

Of course it might just have been a coincidence. But they had never seen it before, and they never saw it again. Neither were there more rats at the school. It may well have simply been an answer to Grace's request. After all, why not?

SOPHIE'S FOOT

Grace had received a fresh understanding of the Holy Spirit in her time in England, and returned to Eritrea with a new expectancy for God to work. It had been tough learning the language during those first five years. She was also trying to cope with training the local teachers, as well as teaching huge classes of kids. In her own words it had been 'One long slog.'

Now, somehow it was easier. But it was still tough. One night as she was in her little hut there was a knock on the door. No one came out after dark, and she wondered who it could be. In limped Sophie, a little Moslem girl. She was dragging one foot that was bleeding and looked badly damaged. She explained that she had dropped a heavy flat iron on it.

Grace and her friend looked at her and sat her down, then got water and tried to wash it. "It's too late to go to the doctor", the friend said, (There was a civil war at the time and a curfew after dark.) "I know," said Sophie, "But I don't want to go to the doctor – I have come to you." Grace took a deep breath and told her that they could pray in Jesus' name for healing. "That is why I came." She said. They closed their eyes, Sophie prayed, and then let out a cry. Grace opened her eyes to find the foot perfectly healed. Nothing crushed. No open wound. No blood. Nothing to see except a perfectly healed foot.

Grace said she never closes her eyes when she prays for healing now, as she was so disappointed not to see the healing happen.

The news was shared everywhere the next day, as Sophie and her mother went around to all their friends and neighbors' telling them again and again what had happened.

It significantly changed how some of the local people felt about 'The foreigners who ran the school'. Somehow gaps were lessened, and there was a closeness that had been absent before. And, not surprisingly, many came for help, and many received it. It was the first of a number of amazing things that opened a whole community to what the God the foreigners spoke of wanted to give them, and He didn't seem so foreign any more. Rather, One who wanted to help them in many and various ways, not just the isolated healing of one young girl's foot.

THE DROUGHT

The area in Eritrea where Grace lived was in the grip of drought. She was running a school of several hundred girls. The situation was dire.

It was severe, all the wells had dried up, the reservoir was empty, the grass had died, the crops had failed, and the land was a dust bowl as were the rivers and water holes. Animals were starving and many died. It was terrible. There had been water on tap that normally provided all the water they needed. Now, when they turned on the tap, absolutely nothing came out. This was true at the school and for everyone else. Getting any supply of water was increasingly difficult.

The government was doing its best to meet the need. Every day big water trucks were sent from the nearest city with water. They came regularly, and people formed long queues to collect their quota from the never-quite-adequate provision. But there were so many people, and folk were so desperate that they should get their supply before it ran out, that it was always a very tense time with much pushing and shoving. And inevitably quite a lot of water was spilled in the frenzy of getting one's own share. Then the buckets or containers had to be got home ... In Grace's words, it was a nightmare.

So Grace and the teachers got together. They believed God would supply their needs. Now the issue was to put it into practice.

As they prayed someone remembered the story of the widow with massive debts and only a little oil left in a flask. That was all she had in the whole house. She had shared her need with the prophet Elijah, and he said she and her sons should go and borrow every jar they could from her neighbors'. Then to come back, and the three of them were to close the door, pour the oil from the flask into the jars, putting them to one side as they were filled. They did, and the oil lasted until all the collected jars were filled. They kept pouring out the oil, and it kept on flowing. Of course it was a much-needed miracle that saved the day for them. The result was that she had enough to pay all their debts and live off what was left.

As they read the story they thought, why, if it has happened before maybe they should try the same? After all, the need was as desperate and the drought as severe. So Grace and her teachers did just that. They collected every container they could, everything that would hold water, even if normally it didn't. Then they laid their hands on the tap, and turned it on. Water started to flow out of it and they collected the water that flowed out. They filled every container they had.

They did the same the next day, and the next, and the next.

Of course the news got out and everyone came to see. They could not understand it as the tap was only connected to the water supply that everyone used, and there was no logical explanation. Some of the men tried every connection between that tap and the place where the water should be coming from. They found no human explanation, because when they looked, there was no water. But, when the staff and pupils prayed, there was the water, flowing as though from a fresh spring.

Of course the school shared its water. Many came to collect it. It continued to flow until the rains came and the drought broke. Then it stopped.

Most were thrilled because they had water. They were so grateful for the provision of their needs, and were interested in something that was so helpful. It broke down many divisions within the community, between different customs, cultures, and faiths.

A SORT OF BIKE RACE

Grace was cycling home from the school she taught in. This was in Asmara, the capital of Eritrea, and Grace lived on the outskirts of town quite a way from the school. A dirt road, mostly uphill on the return journey, was the road she took every day and she knew it backwards.

She was thinking a thousand thoughts, as one does after a day's teaching, but that day she gradually became aware that she was being followed. Usually no one went that way at that time of the day, school closing earlier than other work places, so she looked around to see who it was. It was a man she did not know. At first she didn't think much about it as they were still passing small dirt turn offs to houses on the little roads leading off the one she was on, and she expected him to turn down one of them.

He did not. He stayed the same distance behind her, and that started to worry her as the tracks to houses either side became fewer, and he seemed intent on following her. She started to go faster, and so did he. She slowed, so did he. It was becoming apparent that he really was following her and she was still quite a way from her destination. There was no one walking the road that she could appeal to, and she could not outdistance him. It was not a good situation.

She started to pray. It did not seem to help, as he stayed

the same distance from her and they were in an increasingly deserted area. Turning around and peddling back was clearly not an answer, nor to divert onto any of the dirt tracks that occasionally lead off into the dust, apparently to nowhere. The only safe option was to head for home, but it was still quite a way away.

Desperately, she began to sing. Anything, and everything, that gave her courage. At least that made her feel better. She glanced over her shoulder. The man did not seem quite so close. She sang louder. He fell back further.

Finally he was so far back that she changed her song choice from ones bringing courage to ones of thanks. The man disappeared.

She arrived home without him seeing where she lived, and she was never followed again.

RETURNING IN STYLE

As so often happens when an established pattern is not adhered to, friction appeared, and increased.

Because strangely or not, as she was to learn, such a new and wonderful thing had a downside. And, particularly when the Holy Spirit is at work. The stories in the Acts of the Apostles make that very clear, and I suppose nothing has changed.

The issue of the Holy Spirit seems always to cause division among groups that have not previously known the reality of His power at work among ordinary individuals. It happened in Eritrea, as some were delighted with the new freedom and power to make a difference, and some were not. There was an attempt to stop this 'new' (old) thing spreading. Grace was put in an untenable position, and had no choice but to resign and return to England.

So, Grace's time in Eritrea had come to end, and she was on her way back to England. Pondering how to return she decided she would like to go by boat. It offered the space to rest from what had been an overfull and very tiring time, to come to terms with the changes and challenges ahead, and the opportunity to look at her options and decide what would be good for her.

And being Grace, she thought outside the box. Looking at all the money she had and making enquiries she found that she had enough money not just to go by boat, but also to do so in style. By that I mean first class. So she got on one of the liners that went around Africa between Europe and the UK, and proceeded to have a wonderful time. About as different as possible from the hot, dry, dusty, and poor environment she had lived in for 6 years. Away from the conflicts and smallness and sadness. Simply time to enjoy and be restored.

She told me that she entered every competition that happened, and won a good many of them. That sounded just like Gracie, who has always been wonderfully competitive. She always laughed as she described this bit of her journey. And, knowing her, it is easy to imagine her enthusiasm and laughter and delight at the fun of it all.

Having a friend living in the Cape, and being curious to see something of South Africa, she arranged to get off the boat in Durban, spend a couple of days there, then get the train down to Cape Town and enjoy herself there until embarking again on her ship when it docked there.

She was in Durban for the weekend and she happened to see a concert advertised that she decided she would really like to attend. It was to be on the Sunday afternoon, and she looked for where she could get a ticket, without success. No one she enquired of could tell her. She went to church in the morning hoping for answers, for it was a Christian musical. But they didn't know either, and said they had never heard about it.

Walking down the wide main street of the city she was talking to the Almighty about her disappointment. "I really wanted to go" she said, "but I can't get a ticket." It was a bright, sunny, windless day as she continued on her way back to where she was staying. She was enjoying the walk and the weather and the space but her disappointment nagged at her, and she found herself looking up in a mixture of longing and despair as she continued her walk. Then a piece of paper fluttered down a in front of her. It said, 'Free ticket to …' and named the concert she was about to miss. "This is nonsense" she thought. "Who is playing games with me?"

Then she thought again. "But, what if God is giving me a ticket?" Half excited, half embarrassed she picked up the ticket and put it in her handbag. She got to the shore, sat on a bench, pulled it out and looked at it again. And again. Was this a strange fraud, or was it the real thing?

Finally she decided that it would do no harm to go with this 'ticket from heaven', and see what happened when she presented it at the venue of the concert, which she did, part in wonder and part laughing at herself.

She produced it at the entrance. It was accepted. She found her very good seat, loved the whole thing, and learned that her Heavenly Father has more ways than she had ever dreamed of, of answering her requests.

She got the train to Cape Town, spent time enjoying the country she did not expect to see again, and continued the voyage back to Europe.

She never forgot the ticket fluttering down in front of her, and how much she would have missed if she had dismissed the moment.

MEETING GRACE

When Grace returned from Eritrea, she moved to Clapham, and began teaching at a school for educationally challenged children.

I met Grace because I was hopeless at navigating. I wanted to go to a meeting at Post Green, a place in Dorset where the Holy Spirit was said to turn up once a month, and the possibility of such a thing intrigued me.

I had read about Him, the Holy Spirit, in the Bible of course, but had not, to my knowledge, known Him personally. I knew He changed people who did know him, the Book made that clear enough, but nothing of the sort had happened to me. So Post Green was my destination, and I had no idea where it was, and I have never been any good at navigation.

I decided to phone someone who tended to know what was going on in the Christian world, and therefore might know this elusive place. Indeed she did, and rattled off directions that I was certain I would not be able to follow. "Do you know someone from London who might be going?" I asked. She gave me a telephone number of someone who lived in Clapham. As I lived in Clapham Old Town that seemed positive so I used it, got Grace, found out that yes she knew Post Green, yes there was a meeting this Saturday, and no, she did not want to drive down with me as she was going by train. It was with great reluctance that she agreed to change her mode of travel and meet me at Clapham Junction at 07h00.

Very quickly I realized that we were not in the same space. I was at the time in charge of an oncology ward in a London hospital, most of my patients were dying and I was depressed. Grace was, on the other hand, remarkably bright for that time on a Saturday morning, and I suspected she was usually so.

She seemed to have a hotline to God that I had never encountered and it made me nervous. I had never met anyone quite like that before.

Thoroughly daunted, I abandoned my journey to Post Green and the Holy Spirit, dropped Grace off at a railway station, I suspect to her relief, and headed back to London. It is the only time in my life that I have had two stiff gin and tonics before breakfast.

On Monday a letter arrived from Grace. She said that she found my life to be incompatible with my professed faith (maybe because I smoked and had a smart red car). I phoned to say that although I understood that, I was really struggling, and desperate for answers. She said she couldn't help me and put the phone down.

It was not an encouraging start to a great friendship, but at least we didn't have rosy illusions about each other.

I continued to try and help the patients in my ward, and to pursue my quest for the elusive Holy Spirit by attending every meeting I could that seemed to expect Him. I kept seeing Grace, but usually at a distance. The Holy Spirit also seemed distant.

Months later at one such meeting, she broke the silence and invited me to go out with her for coffee. I was both startled and surprised, as I was sure she had written me off as a disaster, but the invitation was there and off we went. Over the very welcome cups, she said that at the meeting she had been sitting next to a woman whom she had known for some months, who seemed deeply committed in her faith and whom Grace was spending time with regularly. But God had very clearly told her, as she sat there, that the woman did not really want Him at all, only attention, and that I, however unpromising I seemed, really did. That was the beginning of our friendship.

THE WIMPY BAR

I hadn't known Grace long when we agreed to meet one evening at the Wimpy bar. We were living at opposite ends of Clapham, so it was conveniently in the middle and easily found.

It was the first time I had eaten at that particular chain. I looked with interest both at the menu and the meals moving past in the hands of the waitresses, chose what seemed the nicest, and we soon began to eat and talk.

Then a woman came in, walked straight up to us and said "Tell me about Jesus." She looked young, attractive and not at all the sort to accost two strangers anywhere, never mind in a Wimpy bar at Clapham junction.

I was amazed and wondered if I had stumbled unawares into the site of an unofficial church, or even, romantically, the underground variety as found in countries hostile to things Christian. Half of me started to ponder these possibilities, and was Christianity so frowned on in England as to warrant the second of my alternatives: after all it was a question I had never heard asked in any of the restaurants I had ever visited. The other half of me listened as Grace and the stranger started to look at who Jesus was and how one might come to meet and follow Him. Clearly this was what she wanted, for the stranger grasped the possibilities Grace was offering, thanked her profusely, and turned to leave.

I couldn't let her go unchallenged. "Excuse me," I said in my politest tone, "Would you just tell me why you came in here and asked us the question you did?"

Her answer has never left me. "I have wanted to find God for ages, and when I saw you as I was walking past I could see that you knew Him."

I still ponder her answer.

AN IRRESISTIBLE CHALLENGE

Life went on. I continued to do whatever I could for my patients and staff in the ward. But I found it all a huge strain, for however much I knew, and however hard I tried to learn more, I was so aware of how little I really knew. Relaxing on the job was impossible.

Grace continued at the school down the road. It was for 'educationally challenged' children, as it was known then. She loved it, and had the only happy class in the school – if the Headmaster was to be believed.

When we could, we went to Post Green to enjoy the music, got to meet interesting people and find out more about the Holy Spirit. It had always been quite clear to me that Jesus laid great store on His presence as the way to empower his people, but I had not experienced much of that myself. I thought life might go on as it was for the foreseeable future. But then the changes started.

Over the months Grace began to get involved with a group called Youth with a Mission, normally abbreviated to YWAM. It was an organization that encouraged groups of young Christians to take their faith out of their community and find somewhere where they could be significantly helpful. Apparently there were those who had taken up the challenge and were going all over the world and, indeed, 'making a difference'. It seemed rather a fun alternative to pop concerts.

Grace's heart for the world had not changed just because she had left Eritrea. So, she made enquiries about this new group, got to know some of the people involved, went to the odd event, and decided she wanted to be part of it. They offered a three months course in Switzerland, with the most impressive lot of speakers – individuals who had done wonderful things, not just talked about them – and she arranged to attend.

I took her out to coffee and lent her my very warm winter coat for the duration.

When she got back she was full of what she had learned. I was impressed with the practicality of it, having got rather tired of endless discussions that went nowhere. She was obviously impressed, and I kept on working at the hospital.

Then Grace heard about the Hippies. That was to change everything.

It was 1972, and the Beetles had returned from their famous trip to their Guru in Nepal. Uncounted numbers had decided to do the trip as well. It was the thing to do then, to express freedom, adventure, just be young, a sort of trial run for the gap year so common in the West today. They set off from their starting points in America, Canada, and all over Europe and headed east. Most began the land journey in Turkey and went through Iran and Afghanistan, and then on by whatever route they chose to their destination, which was Kathmandu.

It sounded great, but then the dark side started to show. Stories were coming back of many falling ill, getting into trouble with authorities, running out of money, and every other problem one could think of. Many seemed just to have disappeared. There was a suggestion that as many as 40,000 a year were unaccounted for, although there were absolutely no reliable statistics. YWAM had a group working in Afghanistan in the capital,

Kabul, doing what they could to find or rescue these young hippies, and they had put out a call for help. Grace heard about it and told me as much as she knew.

We checked out with a local branch of the organization and, yes, what we had heard was true. We both felt prompted to go. Grace gave up her teaching job at the remedial school, and I resigned from my position as ward Sister in a London hospital, and we got ready to go.

We thought it would be quite straightforward. It turned out not to be.

WHY DRIVE

Having understood that we were going to Kabul to help the hippies, the next question was how to get there. Grace said we should pray about it. I was quite happy to do that, although not at all certain what would constitute a recognizable answer. So I set out to try and find out whether British Airways or Air France was the airline of choice. Really, my mind did not stretch beyond those two alternatives.

Annoyingly, every time I tried to concentrate on obtaining the answer a song kept singing itself in my head, or rather the opening line did. Just the first five words actually, but with the rather nice tune attached. 'Trains, and Boats, and planes', kept thwarting my efforts. Finally I looked up in frustration and said to heaven, "What has this got to do with getting to Afghanistan? There are no trains or boats that go there …" The answer came back, "No, there are not, and I do not want you to go by plane either."

That being settled I went out and sold my beloved car for a much more appropriate, very nice, and not nearly so beloved Ford Cortina Estate, with heavy-duty suspension and a low compression engine. I was assured that it would be more than enough for the job, and so it was … Just for good measure the agent threw in snow chains just in case we would need them. (Only with a navigational error of huge proportions was that a reality, but it was such a nice thing for him to do, and they might have helped us out of mud if we had been able to put them on.)

My next visit, to the Automobile Association, was more problematic. The efficient man serving me assured me the trip was out of the question. Of course, people did do it, and, of course, the car was adequate. But – it seemed insurmountable for him – it was unthinkable to him that I was up to the task. Finally persuaded that I was going to try, he committed, with the gallantry this organization often shows, to giving me the best chance he could for success. We accumulated maps, information, a first aid kit; something called a *carnet de passage*, and the warning that the AA did not provide a rescue service where we were going.

I really felt we were getting somewhere. After all we had a car, and everything the AA could think to offer, to help us on our way. Then mother dropped her bombshell. "What ever you do," she said, "You must not go by car." Her reasons given ranged from the Cossacks in Russia, (not a route that had occurred to us) to snow in the mountains (we had snow chains), with every conceivable trouble and hazard in between. Overwhelmed by this growing cascade of prophecies of doom I retreated to my room to think.

It did seem clear that we should go by car. Equally, to submit mother to weeks or months of anxiety seemed unfair. It looked irreconcilable. Then the thought came. She is doing this because she is afraid for you. That made sense. So did the next thought. Say to the mountain of fear "Be removed and cast into the sea." There was nothing to lose in giving it a go, so I did.

When I went down to breakfast the following morning I found mother going through her picnic basket. It was a particularly lovely one and had been a wedding present. But it was March, raining, and mother did not really go for picnics. I looked at her questioningly. "I thought you might like to take this with you." she said.

After a happy breakfast she showed me the other things she had got out for us to take on the trip. Tea, always useful for trading – a gem of knowledge remembered from her uncle and aunt who had spent most of their adult life in the Far East. Sardines and corned beef, so good when it was hot, Bovril, dried fruit, jam, another first aid kit, the supplies kept coming. She provided the bulk of what we took.

Never again did she mention her misgivings about our mode of transport. In fact I was intrigued to hear her reassuring another member of the family that of course we were going to be all right, we were only going to Afghanistan and we had been to the AA.

It was wonderful what a simple prayer accomplished, and I had a fresh insight into problem solving.

FINALLY WE SET OFF

It was good to finally start the trip that had been so central to our lives since we decided we really were going to do it.

We had done all the collecting of maps and a lightweight tent and camping stuff. We had carefully packed the abundant supplies mother had provided. We had two first aid kits, and the equivalent for the car. We had torches and a whistle and some other of the multiple suggestions people had offered us. We had the AA maps, handy hints, and the all-important *Carnet de Passage*, which, at least theoretically, meant we had car insurance for the whole journey. We had some currency for most of the countries we thought we would be travelling through, and some travellers' cheques. We were as ready as we ever would be. So we left.

We hit our first problem shortly after leaving the house in Clapham, I got to the end of the road and asked "which way?" to Grace. She said, "Right," so I turned. But not, as it happened, right. I have always been slightly confused on that one. So we developed the habit of saying "your side, or my side," which worked perfectly

We set off for Dover, crossed the Channel and had no problems at all once we got used to driving on the left. A large reminder stuck on the steering wheel helped, and we got the knack of roundabouts surprisingly quickly. We stayed in

Campsites, vastly better than the British ones of the time, and met a lot of interesting people. We also got quicker and better at putting up our little tent, getting meals, and reversing the process and getting the tent into a neat bundle in the car.

Our abiding impression of the trip through Northern France was divided into two. We loved the small towns and the beautiful farmland, the ancient old villages, the challenge of seeing traffic lights carefully concealed by overhanging branches, and wonderful food in quaint shops.

However we were reduced to silence with the number and size of military graveyards we passed. The reality and tragedy of war silently screamed at us as we saw thousands upon thousands of white crosses marking the final resting place of as many men. It certainly put any danger we might face into perspective.

We headed on to Switzerland and the YWAM center Grace had stayed at. They made us most welcome, raised an eyebrow at the thought of us driving all the way, and then seized the opportunity of giving us a whole lot of Bibles and stuff to take with us.

WATERMELON

We had had a wonderful few days driving without having to rush, and reached Southern Italy. It had been great to see so many beautiful places, and the time we had given ourselves to get there had proved more than adequate, so we really had enjoyed the trip. We were nearly at the southern tip of Italy, and had spent the night at a nice campsite. We had booked for the ferry from Brindizi to Igiometzia in Greece, done all of our washing and were looking forward to our drive across Greece. As a last activity before we left the site we emptied what was left of the water we were carrying and filled the containers with fresh water from the tap clearly marked as such, filled our thermos with hot coffee and set off. It was not far to the port and we made it easily. No problems that far. They were ahead.

The queue at the docks was considerable and the day very hot. So hot, in fact, that we had used what was left of our Italian lira on cool drinks. After sitting there for some while we reached for the thermos, poured our coffee, and encountered the problem we had no idea we had. The so-called 'fresh water' was in fact seawater, and not only undrinkable but, as there was a cholera scare in the area we had been staying in, not safe either. There was nothing to do but thirst it out until we got on board and could use our Greek drachmas. The queue suddenly seemed a lot longer.

"What we need is some water melon," said Grace, breaking a considerable hiatus. I greeted her statement with silence. Undeterred she went on about how good watermelon was when one was thirsty. I had never even seen a watermelon, but Grace knew all about them and their merits from her years in Eritrea. We had no money, there were no shops in sight, and the only answer I had was to approach my increasingly acute thirst with traditional British stoicism. It was very hot, I did concede that, yes, this unknown watermelon would be lovely. Talking about it was not, in my view, helpful.

Suddenly there was a tap on the car on Grace's side and through the open window came a large slice of something. Grace said, "Watermelon! How lovely, thank you so much". I said "How much?" for, of course; anyone handing out watermelon in those circumstances had to be selling it. But the person had gone. Another slice of this fruit appeared at my window. I was so stunned that I just took it and looked at it as though it might turn into a fairytale carriage … Then I turned to say thank you but the person had gone.

As we savored our miracle fruit the man behind us in the queue came to the window. "Where did you get that melon from?" he asked in broken English. Grace said "A man came and gave it to us. He went that way," pointing down at the docks towards town. The man said, "I know that, but when I saw him give it to you I went after him. When I got to the end of the road he had vanished, and there was nowhere he could have gone."

To this day I do not know the answer. Was he a particularly fleet-footed man? Was he an angel? Why did he come only to our car in the middle of the queue? Why did he bring watermelon? I do know we enjoyed the watermelon whatever the explanation.

I also know that the simple incident, which was not even necessary as we were not in danger of dying of dehydration, did an awful lot to boost my not-so-great faith for when we really did need help later on.

And for the rest of my life, that miracle, and those that happened on the journey ahead, have helped me to look to God for help rather than to panic in trouble or fall into despair.

TURKEY

We caught the ferry from Brindizi to Igiometzia and saw another side of Greece, not part of the average tourist trip at all. We drove more or less due east, adapting to the local pace which was simply wonderful, not least because it was cherry time and we enjoyed them as we bought frequent bag fulls from the side of the road. We went through nowhere of note except the outskirts of Thessalonika, and pondered Paul's travels. My abiding memory was of wonderful trees and a Greece that was very different from the one most visitors encounter.

One morning we were startled to realize that we had reached the eastern point of Europe, and were about to enter Turkey. Of course the western part of it was still, geographically, Europe, but different it was, even so. The music was different, and the signs were mostly in Arabic, though there were enough English ones to make it easy. The shops and markets and street stalls offered food and spices and clothes both familiar, and increasingly not known to us, and sometimes it was hard to keep driving rather than surrender to a few days of sight seeing. There were long stretches between towns however and we saw wonderful old villages with their squares and shops and eating places – something of another world.

One memory is of stopping to get petrol at a roadside garage. As we got out of the car to ask for petrol, we were relieved that the man who was serving us understood our request. Another came and led us to a table and produced coffee. We were joined by two others, and they began to talk with us. Grace had rudimentary Arabic, and they English, and we enjoyed a long conversation together. It was such a wonderful surprise – more like finding friends in an unexpected place than strangers meeting. Then we went back to the car to find that, not only was it full of petrol, but that they had washed it free of its thick layer of dust and also cleaned the inside. They laughed at our amazement, we shook hands, and left delighted. It was one of those unexpected incidents that light up life.

It also balanced the trauma of our first night in the country. We had miscalculated the distance to the next town. It was late, getting dark and difficult driving conditions. So we drew into a lay-by, drew the curtains around the windows, prayed (hard) for protection, and fell asleep almost immediately. Only to be woken up by loud knocking on the windscreen. It was the Turkish police, who had managed to see our car before the bandits arrived. They demonstrated most graphically that we were anything but safe there and pointed us down the road to the next town, the one we thought too far to get to. No longer! We thanked them as well as we could and battled on to it. We could find nowhere to stay so parked at a petrol station next to the pump. Maybe any would-be robbers thought we had run out of petrol, but we were untroubled for the rest of the night. We did our best to make a town each night after that, and saw some lovely cities.

We found Turkey beautiful beyond our expectations, as we drove along stunning valleys with lovely mountains. It seemed unspoilt and very peaceful. We even saw a golden eagle sitting on a rock quite close to the road. It didn't fly off in alarm but calmly watched us pass by. We also caught sight of the snow topped Mount Ararat of Noah's ark fame. Apart from our first night, we had the most peaceful time. A good break before we moved on into more testing territory

RIDICULUOUS GUIDANCE

Our progress east was being decidedly hampered by the rain, a downpour that reminded us we were not (hopefully) that far from Mount Ararat! But at least the road was tarred and in a reasonable state. All was well under the circumstances, until we came to a T-junction. In front of us was a sizeable hill, perhaps even a mountain if we could see it all. The obvious direction was to the right, for the tar went that way. The road to the left was not tarred, looked like any un-tarred road and definitely not first choice.

Why did we hesitate? Well, when we were planning to drive to Kabul we felt God say clearly to us, "When you have a choice, ask Me first." So we did. I confess I was really saying to Him "Of course You want us to turn right ..." But He did not. I felt embarrassed when I gave my answer to Grace, who smiled and said she had heard the same. That, at least, was reassuring. We were to turn left!

So we turned left. It took us hours to get round that mountain. For indeed, it was a mountain of some considerable girth. Visibility was poor, the road was narrow, the drop to the left frightening, and the downpour continued. Our speed was dead slow and it was a question of constant alertness from both of us. The one good thing was that no one else seemed to be on the road, so we didn't need to negotiate cars or lorries forcing us nearer the alarming edge on the passenger side.

Finally we got to the place where our road joined the tar one. We halted in amazement. We could turn left again and join the tar. But behind us there was about 100 yards of tar and then simply a landslide that covered the road as far as we could see. The whole road had been swept away and all we could see were boulders and earth and absolutely no way through.

We will never know whether, if we had turned right we would have come across it and had to turn back, or would have got caught by it and disappeared under the rubble.

I do know we said a profound "Thank You" to God, both for His saying "turn left" and for telling us before we started to ask Him which way to go.

THE BORDER AND
THE BISCUITS

Again and again on this trip we saw how God had known what was going to happen, and what we would need to get through what did.

On our journey eastwards, we came to the border between Turkey and Iran. It seemed intimidating, to say the least. The road went through a narrow pass in the mountains, and there was a furious thunderstorm overhead at the time. Memories of stories of Victorian explorers came unbidden into my mind. They had written about the dangers of such trips, but that was another time, another century, and therefore things were probably safer now, except, at this moment, their warnings and misgivings seemed all too real.

We arrived at the border post looking as tidy and bright as we could. Grace stayed with the car, and I headed for the customs and immigration building, which seemed down an unnecessarily long track, and I soon lost sight of the car. The impressively uniformed officer looked briefly at the passports I offered him, which he stamped. Then he asked to see our insurance. We had got this from the AA in London and it was an impressive looking document in two languages. I was quite proud of it. He was not, and said that we needed additional insurance to cross his country. No amount of pointing out how adequate and reliable and certain the deal offered by the AA was made any difference. He wanted us to get more. I would have, cheerfully, just to placate him, but not at his price which was 200 British pounds sterling, which was a lot of money in those days. It was altogether too much for a two-day drive across the country. In fact it was what we planned to live off for a month. We simply could not afford his insurance.

He was evidently not pleased. "Show me your car," he commanded and stalked behind me as I nervously headed back to Grace and the offending Cortina. She gave him a beaming smile as he circled the car in a manner that resembled a shark about to seize its victim. Clearly he was looking for something to use against us. He inspected the luggage in the boot, and could find no fault. "Open this door," he rasped at us. Grace instantly did, and out tumbled the tin of chocolate biscuits. Its lid came off as it fell, and the whole tinful of melting biscuits fell onto his immaculately shining black boots. I was appalled. Grace looked as though she was trying not to laugh at the outraged expression on his face, and hastily bent over and tried to clean the chocolate off with a handkerchief. There was a long silence. Then he told us, with icy fury, to leave.

We did so as fast as we could. It took a time for our pulse rates to begin to run at normal levels, as a thousand 'What ifs' went through our minds. We blessed my mother.

The reason we had those biscuits was that she, once she got used to the idea of her daughter traveling through central Asia by car, entered into things with real commitment. She had filled boxes with tins of sardines and corned beef, raisins and nuts, salty biscuits, concentrated cool drinks, first aid equipment, water purifying tablets, and other things too numerous to mention. They were all compact and very comprehensive and we were very impressed by her choices. She had also given us quantities of tea, for her Great Aunt Matilda had lived in what was then called Siam for decades, and had told her that it was terribly useful to barter with if there was a problem with cash.

We had, however, wondered about the chocolate biscuits. They were in a tin, in which they were safe, and we from them as they melted; but it seemed an interesting choice given the heat of the journey.

Then we began to laugh. Mother had helped us in ways she would not have dreamed of, as we had not either, and never have we been so grateful for soggy, melting chocolate biscuits. It was with huge gratitude that we thanked God for such un-likely deliverance from a tricky and disconcerting situation.

TOWARDS TEHRAN

We left the official and the tin of biscuits and thankfully headed east through some of the most beautiful and remote countryside I have seen. There were scattered collections of houses grouped together, and the odd town. Otherwise it was the occasional car or truck but mostly just road. We had found out, from the AA and our conversations with people who had some knowledge of the route, that we needed to fill up with petrol whenever we could, as the petrol pumps were often a long way from each other, and the stations did sometimes run out of fuel. And to make sure we found an inn to stay in well before dusk. The man from the ever-helpful AA had also told us that BP had strategically placed pumps along the route we were planning, with camp sites next to them. (They turned out to be a tap and space mostly, but we were grateful for all help offered.)

We quickly adapted to the road and the silence, and enjoyed the journey to our first town, Tabriz. We found a hotel with what looked like a very safe place to leave the car, so, having prayed around it (a habit we have maintained ever since), we had the pleasure of a room and a bathroom for a change.

The next morning we headed towards Tehran. By then we had gotten used to sleeping in the car. Unlike Europe, where the camp sites provided safe camping and car parking enclosed by fences, we had only managed to find rather less secure places to stop further east, and we could not afford to have the car stolen. That really would have been a long walk somewhere ...

When we arrived in Tehran, we managed to find the place where the folk from YWAM had said we would find help. A small group of westerners lived in a house with a lovely view of the magnificent Elburz mountains, which lay between the city and the Caspian sea. It was great to have a bedroom to sleep in, a shower to get refreshed in, and to be made so welcome. The group asked us to stay a couple of days, which we agreed to with great delight. My memory of the city is of the most beautiful roses, and the most hair raising driving I have ever encountered, beyond imagining or description.

The evening before we left, we were approached by some people from the local church. Apparently two young women from Scandanivia had arrived that day. They were heading for the same group in Afghanistan as we were, and had been travelling by bus. Both had health issues, both were ill, and they needed help badly. They didn't want to return home, and it seemed clear we were the best option available. So we rearranged the car and had two new passengers.

I NEED A MAN
WHO SPEAKS ENGLISH

We had left Tehran early the next morning. It had rained hard all night, but was clearing. The road was good, and so was the time we were making. The scenery was quite beautiful, and we were really enjoying it. Until, that is, we came to a bridge that had been swept away in the night's rain. Ahead of us was a line of vehicles, and an impossible way forward. So, we turned back towards Tehran, drove over the beautiful Elzburg mountain range north of the city, and headed for the Caspian Sea. It was a wonderful morning, with fantastic panoramic views and we enjoyed the unexpected delight of it all. But it was a detour of some five hours.

When we finally got to a pretty town by the sea we stopped for petrol. It should have been a simple matter, but for reasons we never understood, it was not. We asked in English and French and by sign language. But the garage attendants just looked at us and shook their heads. With a tank nearly empty, and no idea where the next garage might be, it was not a happy moment. We had no idea where the next garage was, or whether we would find them any more helpful. Was the problem that we were women? It could not be that they did not understand what we were asking for. In my despair I said, "What I really need now is a man who speaks English."

I must have said it out loud. A voice behind me said "Will I do madam?" We were stunned. From where had this elderly gentleman with a cultured English accent appeared? He asked what the problem was, and we told him.

He spoke to the attendant in his own language with a fluency that was impressive. Our car was not only filled with petrol but was being cleaned as well. Clearly this was a man with influence. I asked him how he had come to be there when we needed him. He said that he had been an officer in the Arab legion all his working life, and when he retired he had decided to stay in the area and with the people he loved. Mostly he was without regret, but sometimes he did want to talk English with someone for whom that was a first language. When he had seen us drive past with the British registration of the car and clearly European occupants, he could not resist following us, and hoped we would stop so he could talk with us. We spent the next half hour fulfilling his wish.

At a natural lull in the conversation he asked us where we were going, and when we said Meshad he told us we had better be on our way. He was right; it took us until the last of daylight to get there. We shook his hand and left. We were an answer to his longing that day, and he was certainly an answer to our need. I wish we had spent longer there.

THE SOLDIER

We had been driving for hours, along a rather featureless semi arid area. We had seen few villages, no towns, and only scattered houses, and passed the occasional flock of animals steered by their shepherds and lots of enthusiastic boys. We knew there had to be a petrol station coming up, for they had been positioned along the routes so that one would reach them before running out of fuel. That was the theory. But we were getting quite low on petrol if the gauge was anything to go by. We dropped our speed to conserve fuel, and hoped the theory was right. Even the shepherds were nowhere to be seen now.

Finally a garage came into view. If we had had a choice, we would have driven on. It looked like a set for a bad western movie, abandoned, derelict, and somewhat hostile, and the nearer we got the more our first impression was confirmed. But we had no alternative so, taking a deep breath, praying hard, and with our best face forward we drove up to the petrol pump. There was only one, and it looked as though it came from that bad western movie.

A man came out of the little shack that was alongside the pump. That was all there was, a single petrol pump and a derelict shack. He wandered towards us at a pace that said he was not in any hurry. There was nothing about him that was in anyway re-assuring, rather the opposite. He looked us up and down, obviously sizing up the fact that we were women, and that the car was foreign and in reasonable condition under the layers of dust that all but disguised its color. He then walked around the car, trying to see what else we had in it. We were grateful that we routinely covered the things in the back of the station wagon with a thick black mat so nothing was visible. Nonetheless his behavior was a lot less than friendly, and he had more on his mind than serving us petrol.

Grace, who had some Arabic at her disposal, greeted him with a smile and indicated that we wanted the car filled with petrol. (What else, I asked myself, would induce us to stop at this sinister set up?) He stared at her and said "Money." When she said "petrol" again he just looked at her. It seemed as if we had encountered an unfortunate stalemate. What made it worse at the time, and funny in retrospect, was that he looked exactly like a bandit in the sort of film the petrol station would also feature in. But the absurdity of the situation was not then as real or relevant as the dilemma we were in. The car was almost out of fuel – we had had to pass a garage that had run out of petrol a couple of hundred kilometers before – and we had no idea where the next one might be.

"Help" was the only prayer I could manage, and that rather weakly.

Then I noticed the man suddenly looking over my shoulder and behind the car at something that had certainly caught his attention. What it was I had no idea, as I was not taking my eyes off him, and remained ready to drive off if we had to.

He moved towards the pump and started to turn the handle that would produce the petrol, and with the other hand was trying, really rather anxiously, to get the petrol cap off. He seemed suddenly to have been galvanized into action. I turned to look behind me. There was a man there, a soldier if his uniform was anything to go by, and he held a rifle pointed at our reluctant garage attendant. "Grace", I asked, "where did he come from?" A good question, as we had seen no one for mile upon mile, and certainly not him as we drove up. He seemed to have appeared out of nowhere – Grace just smiled, as though I should have known the answer – but, how very good for us that he had, and that he was clearly on our side in this encounter.

The tank was filled, the money handed over, and the attendant rushed back into his shack and slammed the door, rather as though this soldier terrified him.

We turned to thank our rescuer. He was not there. People sometimes ask who he was. As he came apparently from nowhere, never said a word and disappeared just as strangely, the best answer we have come up is perhaps he was an angel.

TRAVELLING THROUGH AFGHANISTAN

We had made it. Our last problem had been at the border between Iran and Afghanistan. Fellow travellers, hippies all, surrounded us. They regaled us with their tales of woe. Some of them had been there for days because of inadequate paperwork, problems because of lack of sufficient funds, or questions about their cars – they said no one just got through.

That was not a happy thought, particularly as our two Scandinavian friends picked up in Tehran were definitely not well and the sooner we made it to the group in Kabul the better. They, perhaps because they looked harmless, perhaps because they were from Scandinavia, had no problem.

But we had the car … We had made an effort to look neat and presentable, and we headed with some trepidation for the desk. I handed over my passport. There was a long silence and then a lively discussion, none of which I understood. Then they smiled at me and said "Mecca, your name is Mecca." I looked blankly back and said my name was Mekie. "Yes", they said, "Mecca". Grace caught the point. They thought that somehow I was connected to the Prophet, or Mecca, or something to do with the Moslem faith. "Smile," she said, so I did. We were ushered in to the senior officials office. He gave us tea, and we had a friendly chat for some time. He could not have been nicer or more attentive and asked if we would like to stay at his home in Kabul. We thanked him but said we had made other arrangements. He took our papers, signed off everything and bid us farewell.

We drove to Herat. There was no alternative route according to the AA in London but the main one, which went first to Herat, then to Kandahar in the South, and then north again to Kabul, so there was no problem about which road to take. Apparently both the Russians and the Americans had built it. The Russians, the short bit from their country to Kabul, including a very impressive snow tunnel for travel in winter. The rest, from the border with Iran to Kabul, via Herat and Kandahar had been built by the Americans, a very long way indeed.

Choosing somewhere to stay in Herat was a matter of doing the best we could, in a land and culture that we knew almost nothing about apart from the fact that a lot of hippies seemed to have got lost on the way. It seemed a lovely city, and it would have been great to have had time to explore it. Instead, we found an unmemorable place and were delighted to have a meal we had not made and somewhere to sleep. We were so tired that my memories of it are almost nil.

Travelling south to Kandahar along countryside and distant Caravans and tents that Abraham would have recognized, we realized we were in a totally different world. We chose an Inn where we could have the car in the compound, and thanked God for the national tradition that protected anyone within the property as long as they did not offend the rules of hospitality. Frankly, it felt as unsafe as anywhere I have been, but we were inside, and therefore safe until we left. We were the only Europeans. From the expressions on the faces of those who gave us entrance, and therefore the guarantee of their protection, we were unlikely visitors.

Our Scandinavian friends, pleading exhaustion, disappeared to their room. Grace and I had opted to sleep as usual in the car so it could not be stolen while we slept. We accepted the invitation to eat. The meal was served in what seemed to be the general meeting place in an ancient place that looked as old as it is possible. We had little common language. Grace's Arabic was invaluable, and otherwise we managed with smiles, shrugs, and saying thank you with all the positiveness we could convey. We ate what seemed like watercress soup, and chops, probably goat, but perhaps camel, and were deeply grateful for their friendliness. I felt as though I had walked into a film set.

It was a long way to Kabul and we set off early. The road remained good and the traffic light. We made it by late afternoon. The city was set on the edge of a mountainside, and our first view was of what seemed endless skulls covering the surface. Eerie is putting it mildly. Of course they were not skulls, but dried earth houses with windows where eyes would be, but the effect was startling. We managed to find the house we were heading for, and joined the team. It seemed we were the last to make it.

Was it worth going by road? A thousand times yes. We had a lot of fun. We saw God help us in amazing ways. And we were able to help a couple of fellow travelers along the way.

KABUL

We were warned of the dangers of walking the streets on our own, or even in two's, and always had to be well covered with clothes. Men went past holding guns that looked as though they had been used in the wars against the English a hundred years before, toting huge daggers in their belts.

The market was a place of wonder, with its donkeys, camels and goats, and produce from out of town farms, and endless unusual clothes and utensils and jewelry and lamps and the wonderful Afghan embroidered leather coats. There was every sort of food as well, and the combined aroma of animals, humans and exotic foods filled the air.

But it was the women who caught my attention the most. They seemed so tall and stood so straight, and were clearly sharing at length with each other, mostly one to one, but also in the occasional larger group. Every one of them was covered from head to foot by a single garment; it looked pleated and strangely made them looked like walking tents. Only their wrists and hands were allowed to be seen but their faces were covered by the 'tent', except for a strip in front of their eyes where a thick woven mesh allowed them to see out enough to get around. It must have been like having a loosely made tapestry base to look through. Of course no one could see what they looked like, which was the point. But it also meant that none of them could ever get an open view of anything at all. I felt such respect for their dignity and grace as they moved from one stall to another. We had been warned not to go into the market, but how we would have loved to have the language and gone to talk with them.

Although we had a car we mostly walked everywhere. The car was useful for transport if folk wanted to use it, and that widened the horizons somewhat. One day we went some way up the famous Kabul pass, and caught a glimpse of the hugeness of the mountains around the Kabul valley, and how very dangerous it would have been to leave the safety of the car. It was wild and unchanged and very tricky to travel on, but offered the route to Pakistan, not that far away. (It was the route of the disastrous retreat by the British from Kabul in the 1800's where only one person, a doctor, made it through. Looking at the terrain it was easy to see why.)

Some of us went to the caves that had been discovered in the mountains on the road north. It was both huge fun, and very frightening.

But, we had not come as tourists.

We were involved in an outreach in Kabul under the YWAM umbrella. They were trying to help the young Western folk (hippies) who were in trouble. They were, at that time, traveling through Afghanistan in vast numbers. All on their way to Katmandu following the route taken by the Beetles. Many never made it, and many died on the way. They came in their cars, or by any of the local busses, or hitch-hiked without any real understanding of the countries they were travelling through, the costs involved, the cultural differences they would face, or the disasters that would befall them.

One of the terrible memories I have is of the walls in one of the hotels they used. They were all covered with photographs sent by parents of those who had started the journey and had not arrived at Katmandu. They all said basically the same thing. "This is my son/daughter. If you see them call this number, collect, we will pay. We want to find our child." Hundreds of individual cries for help.

The team tried. We went to the hotels. We spoke to whomever we could. We prayed. We helped some. One of the big problems was that drugs were so cheap. After all Afghanistan is a major producer of Heroin. So getting one's drug fix there cost a fraction of the cost elsewhere.

Grace was a lot better at communicating with these desperate young people than I was, but for everyone it was a bit like trying to stop the tide coming in. I found my hope of personal effectiveness sinking beneath the waves quite quickly. I realized that I was not fitting in to the group, and wondered if there would ever be a group for me.

All my uncertainties and insecurity flourished and in fact, I felt that my sense that my newfound faith would lead me overseas was probably wrong. I resigned myself to going back to England and forgetting my dreams. I still hoped that maybe, somewhere, there was a place for me in the wide world I longed to be part of. One day I made a plea to God. We were due to make the long trip back to the UK via Munich and the Olympic games the following Monday. I asked Him to make it unmistakably clear before we left if He wanted me ever again to venture beyond the cliffs of Dover. Otherwise I would put aside my hopes and longings and do my best to settle back in the land of my birth. I don't know if I feared an answer more than not having one.

I gave Him until Sunday to do so.

AN UNEXPECTED ANSWER

The days past quickly and finally it was Sunday. I had always thought that would be the easiest time for Him to get through to me, but the day passed with silence. We went to the evening service at the local and only church. I had little hope of any word from heaven on the matter at hand.

My quiet cloud of despair was suddenly penetrated by the arrival in the pulpit of a woman who commanded attention. I had distantly heard the church pastor introduce her as Darlene Rose but nothing had prepared me for what was about to happen.

The entire congregation was riveted before she spoke a word. She looked slowly around the church and then said, "If you have raced with men on foot and they have worn you out, how can you compete with horses? If you stumble in safe country, how will you manage in the jungle of the Jordan?" The quote from Jeremiah was one I had never noted, but have never forgotten.

I knew, with that knowing that knows, that this woman understood about living in circumstances that were beyond her ability to cope, and that she had come through all that life had flung at her, victorious. I listened with total attention.

She told her story, simply and without emphasis. She spoke of being a missionary in Borneo, and of all the danger and cost of being the first white woman to live among a Stone Age tribe.

She told us about being imprisoned by the Japanese during the Second World War, of interrogation and torture that turned her hair quite white when she was in her twenties. She spoke of her husband dying, a prisoner in another camp some distance away, and her overwhelming sense of loss, of fighting off rabid dogs, of slow starvation and the terror of the camp being bombed by the allies.

She told us of the long time she had spent recovering her health, and then returning to the same tribe she had first worked in. It was the stuff of hero's.

Yet, she conveyed that it was God, not her, who had made it all happen, had given what was needed to emerge victorious, to cope, to be effective when it was far more than all too much.

Suddenly, mid-sentence it seemed, she stopped, looked straight at me and said, "I want you to know that, whatever it costs to go on, it will cost more to go back." She said it again, although she did not need to. I heard it the first time, and I was, and remain, satisfied with the answer. It convinced me that I should stop looking at how things were going, and focus instead on trying to follow Jesus, learn better how to become more like Him, and simply do what I thought He was showing me. He would provide the ability.

She never knew what her words meant to me. I thank God for her often, and pray for her also. It was one of those rare God moments that change forever the person who has them.

I have got it wrong often, and changed far more slowly than I hoped. But I have never been tempted to give up, even in moments when I could only stand still as I did not know how to go on. That reality was settled for me all those years ago in a distant church in a far away land.

So I had my answer; my need was met.

ACHMED, THE COOK

The best thing for us in the entire stay happened on our last evening before starting the long journey back. Instead of the normal evening meal, we were given a full English one, roast beef, roast potatoes, green peas … everyone was a bit surprised.

Grace and I were really touched; for somehow we suspected Achmed our cook had done it for us because we were the only English people there and we were leaving. Afterwards we went to say thank you.

"I am glad you came", he said. He went on to tell us his story. He and his wife were devout Muslims, with a great hunger for God. So much so that they did everything they knew to find the peace they lacked. They had even given their firstborn son to a childless couple to earn merit, in the hope that that would fill the emptiness they felt. But it hadn't.

When Achmed got the job working for the foreigners, his wife said to him, "Look carefully, perhaps they have what we seek." And everyday when he went home he had said, "Not today." "But when you came", he said, "I went home and said to my wife that two women who spoke English differently had come in a car. And that you were different."(Most of the YWAM team came from the USA, and the rest from Europe.) "My wife told me to watch carefully; perhaps you had what we were seeking. So I have watched. And every night I told my wife what I had seen and we talked and hoped. And we wanted you to know, before you left, that we have found the peace with God that we have looked for, for so long."

We were stunned. We had not noticed his watching us, nor had we had much conversation. But, I would have walked to Kabul if it had meant this would happen, and it transformed the trip for me. Others in the team had been helpful to the Hippies. We might have been, but to be the answer to Achmed's cry was more than enough to make the journey for. To this day I am amazed by the wonder of it. God used us to reach this family regardless of how we, particularly I, were feeling, or our unawareness of our effect on Achmed.

ALL THE WAY BACK

It was time to return home. We repacked the car, said our goodbye's and set off on the long trip back via Munich and the Olympic games. Of course it helped enormously to have travelled the road one way, because, until we left Turkey we simply had to take the same road back, and this time we had an idea where the petrol stations were and where we might stay.

All was going well. We had left Kabul behind and were heading along the road to Kandahar. Then two things happened in quick succession. I was stung by what seemed like a bee or a hornet. Grace got rid of the insect, and there seemed no problem beyond a bit of pain. Then I lost my sight. The world simply went black, and I could see nothing at all. I did not feel ill, simply stunned at the blindness.

We stopped, of course. We prayed, naturally. We made some tea and drank it (how English can one be). Then we decided to go on, with Grace doing all the driving. It was one of those awful times when one can only do what one can and it did not feel enough.

Grace drove on, and did everything with great confidence. I tried to stay cheerful and be positive and chat when Grace wanted it. We both prayed hard as this was not a great scenario. The good thing was I didn't feel ill, just thrown and blind. Then, some hours later, perhaps five, maybe seven, my sight came back. Just like that. It was one of life's wonderful moments, following one of the most frightening.

Was that a reaction to the bite? Had I been cursed? Was it an unknown illness? All we did know was that we were back on track again and reached Kandahar safely.

WHO NEEDS A HAND BOOK

We were somewhere in Central Asia, on the way back to Europe. I could now see, which was still wonderful! We were enjoying the scenery, had been watching on our right some distant tribe on the move with endless camels, donkeys and assorted animals. We knew not to get close, as we had had a bullet hit us on the journey out, fortunately from a distance that made no more than a hole in the side of the car.

Then, without warning the engine died and the car rolled to a stop. It was not a great place for it to have done so. That wandering tribe of herdsmen suddenly seemed much closer, and we knew we were far short of the next small town. I felt very vulnerable.

But there was no time for self-pity. I knew Grace was better at praying than I was so I suggested she did that while I had a look at the engine. I opened the bonnet with a desperate prayer for help. We had lots of spare parts, recommended by the ever-helpful AA, as well as a sizeable book telling us, step-by-step, what to do in almost any emergency. But I understood almost none of it and had no time to sit down and read ... I gazed somewhat blankly at the silent engine.

Suddenly the thought came, "Put that on that." Somehow I knew what the 'that's' were. Picking the moveable one up I moved it onto the other 'that'. It fitted, so I closed the bonnet, got back into the car and switched on the engine. A reassuring noise filled the car, and we drove off just as the first of the wandering tribe appeared over the not-so-distant hill.

After some minutes Grace said to me "What did you do?" I told her. "What was the 'that?" she asked. I admitted I had no idea.

She smiled and said it clearly did not matter, as we were fine again, and that was actually what mattered.

Then she suggested that I never mentioned this incident when there were men in the group ...

WONDERFUL PROVISION

The next day we were in Herat, and then drove into Turkey, which is one of the loveliest countries I have been in. We made far better time because we knew the road somewhat, and so were able to bypass places because we knew we would easily make the next. Finally we crossed out of Turkey and were back in Greece. It was good to be back in Europe.

We had not been to Yugoslavia on the trip east, so we camped quite near the border, and crossed over after breakfast the next day. We were heading for a town where we needed to get some local currency when we saw two men pushing a car along the other side of the road. The car looked full, loaded with two ladies and children, so it was far from easy for them. It was also quite a way to the next town so we stopped and asked if we could help. They had run out of petrol they said, so we got one of our spare cans out and offered them some of ours. They offered to pay us, we said no it was good to be able to help, and then one of the men stuffed notes in our hands anyway. We all hugged each other, and went our separate ways.

Some time later we arrived at the first largish town to visit a bank and get some local currency. They were all closed. All of them. Apparently it was a public holiday in Yugoslavia that day and we would find no bank open until the next day. But we did find out as we asked a man who spoke some English that the money we had had stuffed into our hand was a lot more than we suspected. Enough for us to stay for the night and get money the next day in a bank quite a lot further north.

We continued our journey, heading towards Vienna, with increasing volumes of traffic, as it seemed we were one of vast numbers heading for Munich and the Olympics. At one point a shepherd was determinedly driving his sheep down the main road, thwarting a number of drivers who found sheep pace more than frustrating, but a wonderful example of life going on even if the traffic couldn't.

THE OLYMPICS

Finally we found Munich, and the castle that YWAM said they were putting us all up in. It really was a small castle, worthy of the name, and surrounded by tents of every size from huge to tiny.

We found ordered chaos as members of the YWAM team arrived in their dozens. The organization had for years seen teams of mostly young people, trying to meet local needs, be useful, and share the answers they had found through their faith in Jesus. It seemed that they had come from all over the world to this event with huge excitement. One of their leaders, Don Stevens, had caught the vision of a team big enough to be significant, and this was the result.

Of course, being in Germany at the Olympics brought back memories of the last time the Games had been held in Germany. It had been in 1936, in Berlin, and memories of Adolf Hitler and his Nazi Party were an unwelcome shadow that everyone hoped would fade as the new Germany was clearly shown to all. Everything the organisers could think of had been done to make it all a huge success, and the results were very impressive.

We spent the short time before the games getting used to the castle. The sleeping accommodation consisted of tiers of bunks just big enough to accommodate an individual. There was little room for anything else, and everywhere was minimal but entirely adequate – and who minded about queuing for everything? (I was reminded of the accommodation prisoners in WWII described, and realized how lucky we were that this was only for two weeks.)

We went into the city by train, and went around some of the huge open spaces and parks, which were thronged with visitors. This was mostly where the young were, as town was expensive, and of course the Games had not started.

The authorities were obviously desperate that no one caused any negative situation, and so our leaders had been given very precise instructions, and pretty tight boundaries. It seemed they thought such a Christian group was potentially a security risk. We spent time chatting, singing, praying and looking at what was going on, and listening to the leaders as they shared their hopes and dreams. We also saw a very large group of those obviously with different beliefs, practicing witchcraft, magic and all sorts of religious rituals as well, which really one would expect. I had not seen such overt demonstration of their beliefs and rituals before. Clearly they were part of the program as we were, and we probably looked odder to them than they to us. In another age they might also have been viewed as a security risk, which highlighted the openness of the Games to all.

Finally the Olympic Games were happening and we loved the vibes and got on with the things we were assigned to, mostly in groups of seven to ten as I remember. I also loved listening to our music groups who were first rate, although we were kept well away from the stadium by the authorities. That made no difference, for we were having a wonderful time meeting every sort of person from just about anywhere.

Then one morning we were told of the Israeli athletes being taken hostage, and things did not look good. The authorities, we were told, wanted us in town as soon as we could get there, to see if we could help in any way. We scrambled for the trains, and did all we could to comfort those in our carriages. Grown men were weeping brokenheartedly as the past reared its awful head. Whereas they had not even seemed to notice us before, now they poured out their shock that this event, which should have demonstrated how far Germany had moved from the past, had instead brought back stark memories, and surfaced buried pain.

It was so hard to see, and we all gave it everything we had, mostly listening and simply being there. Then we got to the great open space. We were in a group that was quite sizeable, and our leader was trying to proclaim the answer Jesus offered. It seemed as though he was getting nowhere. Then Grace quietly said, "I think we should all turn inwards, give all our attention to God, and sing." We promptly did so. It was one of those all too rare moments when it seems as though Heaven opens and there He is. We all felt the change, we sang with all the comfort He gave us, and people started to come from all over the place and ask for prayer and help and tell their stories and ask for healing.

The outcome politically, and for the poor captives, was not good. The athletes were murdered, a lot of blood was shed, and a dream broke. But there was also a lot of good sharing and the opening up of hurts, old guilt, the chance to be heard and understood and a coming together that was as profound as it was unexpected.

When we left to go back to London it seemed such an anticlimax, yet all I can remember is how very good it was to be going back home.

A FOLLOW UP
ON AFGHANISTAN

About ten years after we left Afghanistan, Grace was on the west coast of America and was asked to address a home fellowship group. She decided to share some of her own and my Afghanistan experiences. Shortly after she started her talk, a woman interrupted her and asked if she was Grace of the Grace and Helen team who went to Afghanistan by car. Grace answered in the affirmative, whereupon this lady explained that there was a young man in the church who was training to be a pastor. Three weeks prior to Grace's US visit she asked him how he became a Christian, and he explained that it was through his encounter with Helen and Grace.

As I was tidying a drawer in the filing cabinet I came across this story in a folder of Graces'. I had never heard the story, I cannot think why not, and it absolutely delighted me. It had been a tough time, and this was such an encouragement, of God doing things beyond what we know …

DON'T BLESS ME

Having left nursing I went back to teaching, which offered more time and freedom, and found myself in what was then called a 'Special school' for children with many different reasons for struggling with education. Some were immigrants who had little or no English, some had learning difficulties, others were hostile to being at school at all and made life all but impossible at times.

Every day was a challenge. Although the classes were small, no more than fifteen in number, the reality was that every child really needed almost constant attention, and some of them needed protection from the hostile ones. Having been used to quite different needs and challenges in the Oncology ward I had come from, I was having to adjust fast. Every day I went home exhausted and thinking there had to be an easier way of making a living. Every day my desperate prayer was for wisdom and the strength to make it to going home time.

And then there was Jenny.

Jenny was thirteen, and had the foulest language I had ever heard, and I had counted as my friends some of the really rough men from the back streets of Lambeth. She didn't only use these words when she was angry, she used them all the time. Perhaps she was always angry, perhaps that was how they spoke at home, I did not know the answer.

The other dreadful thing was she had bad breath. I don't know if she ever cleaned her teeth, but the awful odour when she opened her mouth carried well beyond the gap between her and the person she was speaking to, and it wasn't only me who found herself walking backwards during any conversation with her.

The only way to describe the dilemma I had with her was that she really got to me. I didn't want to see her, hear her, be in the same room with her, or even the same building. I simply did not know how to cope.

So I did the only sensible thing I could think of doing; I asked God how to handle this. I didn't want to show my feelings; the poor girl probably had a difficult enough life, but they were dangerously near the surface.

"Bless her," He said. "Are you serious?" I asked.

Apparently He was, and that phrase *bless those who curse you* came to mind. I was not at all sure what was going to happen, but give it a go I would.

No sooner had I reached the corridor next morning than there she was, and she started to harangue me, same words, same lack of toothpaste. I took a deep breath.

"Bless you Jenny," I said. "What did you say?" was her astonished retort. "Bless you" I repeated. A long silence followed. "Listen Miss, if I don't curse you, will you stop blessing me?" "Goodness, this thing works!" was my silent response. She interrupted my silence with a desperate repetition of her plea. She couldn't stand me blessing her she said. I said that, if she did not curse me, I would not bless her. We parted mutually stunned by our conversation.

She never cursed me again. Often she opened her mouth, and then rapidly shut it. Sometimes we got as far as a few words in normal language.

I never audibly blessed her again, but I have prayed for her many times since.

WHAT NEXT

Grace and I were back from Afghanistan and had moved quite soon afterwards to Dorset where we were teaching in a local school, wondering 'What next?' For it was clear to us that, not only was there a 'next,' but also it would be overseas. As we thought and prayed it became clear that the answer was South Africa. (I thought that wonderful, as, in 1972, we could hardly make it worse. The news of increasing trouble and the inevitable escalation of it until some sort of handover of power to the majority occurred was inescapable.)

So we taught for another eighteen months, saved hard, had a wonderful time at the ancient local church at Canford, and got ready to go.

On the way down to Southampton and the ship, we passed under a brilliant triple rainbow. I have always loved them, mostly because they remind me that God keeps His promises. We certainly needed that reassurance.

The journey to Cape Town took three weeks. Grace took to life at sea like a duck to water, won most of the competitions that were held, and got involved in everything going.

I discovered, as I got seasick before we got fully into the English Channel, that this was not my favorite way of travelling, but did my best to enjoy as much as I could, reminding myself that Admiral Nelson also got seasick so there was no shame in it.

THE CAPE TOWN ERA

It was wonderful to reach Cape Town, although we only realized we were doing so as the ship started to slow, for we were on the wrong side of the ship – the stunning sight of Table Mountain towering over the city was blocked completely. I understood in a new way the significance of the word 'posh'. It was the code for 'Port Outward and Starboard Home.' Apparently in past eras all the rich people chose those sides of the ship so they could see the land through the windows as the ship made it's way around Africa and then to India, while the poorer gazed endlessly out at the sea, and missed the views.

Getting off and extracting our luggage was fun.

We found the kind lady, a friend of a friend of Grace's, who had come to pick us up. Fortunately we had little luggage as three of us plus luggage filled the car. We drove excitedly down the peninsula to Diep River. Our new friend announced proudly on arrival that she had only passed her driving license the day before and that had been her first solo trip. How very brave of her to do so.

The following day we went into town and bought a second hand car. Beautiful it was not, but it was affordable, it worked, and we needed it.

We also started to find out what we didn't know. The notice over the public ladies toilets said *Slegs Blankes*. We understood the *Blankes* bit as, at that time Apartheid, with all it's nightmare racial restrictions was in full flow, but did *Slegs Blankes* mean only white or no whites?

We felt pain at the question, and had to wait for someone to go in to get the answer.

Then signs on the road, which also directed us in a language we had yet to attempt, and driving which was very different and took some adjusting, confronted us.

When Saturday came, Grace said we should pray about which church to go to. I found myself thinking of the various denominations on offer until Grace announced with certainty "St John's". So we found out where a St John's was and went. It was an old garrison church in Wynberg, large and impressive, of the old English Anglican style, and about a third full. We enjoyed it enough to go to the evening service. To our surprise the Rector stopped us as we were leaving, asked us our names, and invited us to lunch the following Sunday.

Over lunch with the Rector, Bruce and wife Joan, we were asked every question they seemed able to think of. So nicely that it was still a great meal. Then he said, to our complete amazement, "Last week something happened that has never happened to me before. I heard God say of you both, 'I have sent them, look after them.'"

He did. He was the one who got us permanent residence. Not without difficulty, as all English speaking 'fulltime Christian workers' were seen as opponents of the ruling Apartheid government and therefore blocked from staying. Grace was granted her permanent residence almost immediately but mine took three years and the recommendation of a cabinet minister before it arrived.

We began to explore the Cape peninsula, went to all the meetings at St John's and anything else we were invited to. A couple of weeks later we were summonsed to the Archbishop's residence in Bishopscourt. His Grace, to give him his correct title, was a tall, very thin man with a lovely smile. He cross questioned us for about an hour about all we had done; Grace's time in Eritrea, our time in Afghanistan, our life and work in England, and just why we had turned up in Cape Town. "You may be wondering why I asked to see you," he said. "I heard about you, and I wondered if you were not an answer to a prayer of mine. You see, God is blessing us with a move of His Holy Spirit. All over the country I am hearing of priests and pastors who talk of His coming, and of speaking in tongues, and of a new dimension in their ministry. I too had such an experience while I was bishop of Grahamstown, before I was made Archbishop of Cape Town. I know God wants us to go on in the Spirit, and I know many out there need help. I am very limited in what I can do, so I have been praying for someone to come and help us. When I heard of you two I thought you might well be God's answer."

That was the last thing I would have thought of. Grace and I simply looked at him with blank amazement all over our faces. "What I want," he continued blithely, "Is for the two of you to accept every invitation you get, and I will make sure you get them. Go wherever you are asked, and help these people who are being touched by God to understand what the Bible says, and encourage them to go on with Him. We need God's power, a church that is alive and helpful, and for the leaders to be able to follow the Spirit."

We became good friends with Bishop Bill Burnett, and with his wife Sheila. Not that we saw a lot of them, for the next few years we seemed to be travelling all over the country most of the time.

THE BEGINNINGS OF AN UNFINISHED JOURNEY

The invitations did indeed come. The first was from a local Methodist church, then from St John's, and on to outlying suburbs around Cape Town and then Beaufort West in the Karoo. Here we met Ozzie and Deidre, the Methodist minister and his wife. They made us wonderfully welcome and told us that we would be addressing the men's monthly meeting the next morning.

Ozzie did warn us that they were not the most responsive of men, but he wanted us to speak anyway. We were grateful for the warning, for it was clear, even before the start of the proceedings, that the men were not thrilled that we were on the program. They started to tell stories, play charades, and discuss local events, quite disregarding the minister's attempts to introduce us. I was quietly sympathetic, suspecting there had been far too many disastrous visitors before us.

Finally, with a whole fifteen minutes to go, we started. Grace had whispered to me as this wonderful battle of wits had gone on, "Tell them about Afghanistan ... I did. Briefly, unemotionally, I told them about going there to help the Hippies, the thousands of young people who were following the Beetles trip across Asia to Katmandu. I spoke of the ones in jail, those dying on the way, of the hundreds of desperate letters on the walls of the hotels where distraught parents begged for news of their children. Of addicts, who could not kick the habit, and how little we could do. Of how desperate and awful we felt as we left.

I stopped abruptly because I could not think of anything more to say. I had spoken for just over two minutes.

I don't know what made me feel worse, the still raw memories of the lostness of the Hippies and those multiple hundreds of despairing letters on the walls of the hotels desperately wanting news of their vanished children, or the futility of trying to communicate with the men around me.

An impossibly long silence followed. It seemed to last for ever. Finally a man stood up and spoke. "When I heard these ladies were coming," he said, "I thought, oh well, be kind to prisoner's week ... But now I realize, I am the prisoner. You are the free ones." He turned to us, apologized for how they had behaved, and then turned back to the group saying, "I have never told any of you that I made a commitment to follow Christ while I was at school. And I still do, but I have been afraid to tell you lest you think less of me." He sat down, and the silence intensified.

Then another man stood up, told of his hidden faith, and sat down. It became a waterfall. They all had been secret disciples, all afraid to say so, and were amazed at what was going on. The relief, emotion, celebration, and the questions lasted long after the scheduled cut-off time.

We learned later that they had all sought out the minister, asked to receive the Holy Spirit, and were all changed men thereafter.

YOU HAVE LOVELY EYES

We were a long way from home. It had taken us about twelve hours of driving to get to where we were going. And all that time I was wondering what we would find when we got there.

The clergyman who had contacted us was unknown to us. Yet his plea was one we could not ignore. He had said that his congregation was going nowhere. It was as though there was a great cloud of unhappiness over the place. He had done everything he could think of. Then he thought of us, for we had the reputation of being willing to go anywhere. It was rather fun to think of us as a last resort.

We arrived a little after we had hoped, and so went straight into meeting the clergyman and some of his team. They had thoughtfully laid on coffee and something to eat. It was quite clear as they talked that the assessment of where they were was, indeed, where they were, dismal!

I haven't often been in a group so quite without hope. I turned to the food, hoping that eating something would give me time to think. Sandwiches. I am quite a fan of sandwiches normally. These were different, for the bread was pink and grey. It was easy to source the pink; the processed meat was full of some sort of dye, but the grey ... Nonetheless, we were being offered food, and I was grateful, if not exactly delighted.

As the meeting went on we began to realize that there was a

woman there who both played a very dominant role, and was also clearly at odds with herself and everyone else. She was also the person who had prepared the sandwiches. But there was no time to do more than notice, for we had to find our host's home, turn around, and get to the first meeting with the congregation. It went surprisingly well given the prevailing mood.

The next day we had a full program and the mood lifted somewhat, for the people who came were deeply committed, and clearly wanting more than they had. The snag was that the dominant lady was so desperate she affected everyone else with her interruptions and comments. We began to suspect she might be the cause of the logjam in the community.

But, the question was what to do about it? Ideas seemed absent. Then a thought came into my mind, and before I had time to think twice I acted on it. "You know, when you smile, you have lovely eyes." I said to her. She looked at me in shock, almost as though I had hit her. There was a long long pause, and then she said, "What did you say?" I repeated it, what else could I do? And, as I took a deep breath, she got out of her chair, turned her back on me and walked out of the room. I took another deep breath, prayed like mad that God would meet her and got on with the next thing.

At lunchtime she came to find me. I was in the middle of a group when she headed straight for me. She had obviously been crying, and I felt quite helpless. Then she said "I was so angry when you spoke to me. No one ever says nice things about me. They never have. I thought how dare you say that? Then something made me go to the ladies room and see if what you said was true. It took me a long time to manage a real smile, for it is so long since I did. Finally I managed, and it is true. When I smile, I do have lovely eyes."

She changed. In front of us all she changed. I cannot say what or how, only that somehow, in the way only God can manage, that highly defended and bruised heart had been touched, and a healing process begun.

We left the next day, having already seen a significant breakthrough in the community, and a definite feeling that spring was in the process of defeating a long, hard winter. I never saw her again.

By the way, when she did smile, she really did have lovely eyes!

THE MOLES

I don't know whether it was the memory of Grace's story of rats in Eritrea that helped to solve the problem of the moles years later. Certainly the association was obvious, but I did not see it.

We were spending our first Christmas in South Africa house sitting for a family in Cape Town. The family who lived there were desperate for someone to do so, and we seemed the perfect answer to them.

All we had to do was keep the house safe and the lawn perfect. Easy enough we thought. Until, that is, we woke up two days later to find molehills, many of them, turning the lawn into a definitely less-than-perfect state. In fact, the damage they had managed to achieve in a single night spoke of either a lot of them, or a frenzied attempt to achieve a world record for mole digging.

Neither of us had too much experience of ridding a garden of moles. We knew we couldn't put down poison for there were two dogs and a cat, and we didn't want to kill them, merely to see the moles gone and the lawn restored to its previous pristine state.

We were stumped. At least I was. That evening I saw Grace walking all around the lawn, talking, I imagined, to herself as she did so. The next morning we found two moles stretched out, dead, on the lawn. I was amazed, but Grace said "Thank

You." Then she told me that she had gone over the lawn the night before saying to the moles under her feet, "Leave or die!"

Presumably the two dead moles were the two that refused to leave. We don't know how many heeded the warning.

We never saw evidence of another mole the whole time we stayed, and were able to hand over a still perfect lawn to the owners.

THE GIFT OF
INTERPRETATION

I had long believed that the gifts of the Spirit were supposed to be used in everyday life as well as in church services, and had seen the benefits they brought often. But this was something different.

We had a regular Bible study group of somewhere between ten and twenty women (of course none of us could come every week), and we enjoyed the free discussion around a chosen passage. It was great fun and we all benefitted in our different ways. Who we were varied as people came and moved on or away. There was a great freedom in that, and a sense that people were there because they wanted to be. Our diversity was also wonderful as we represented a wide spectrum of views, and therefore enriched, encouraged, and challenged each other.

A new lady joined. She may have been one of the original hippies if one looked at her clothes and her car, or a member of an artist's commune in Paris, or simply a very different person. We all really valued her being part of the group for she had the kindest face and gentlest ways, and clearly loved being part of us. The different thing about her was that she was very quiet, and we were a fairly noisy group. Quiet as in not saying anything, for months. Then she began to contribute, and we saw a different side of her silence. We, and by that I mean all of us, were not at all sure what she was saying.

In one way it was not an issue as everyone felt free to contribute – sometimes it would be part of the debate, sometimes just a comment that needed no response, or a point that took the group in a new direction. We never felt pressured to get it right all the time, that would have defeated the freedom and adventure we had, but mostly we understood more or less what was said, whether we agreed or not.

Not so with our new friend. It seemed as though she never finished one sentence before moving on to another, on a different train of thought. It didn't matter unless she wanted more of a response than a smile and a thank you. There had to be an answer.

It came. "Use the gift of interpretation" was the instruction as we prayed. So when she spoke the answer was, "In other words ..." And it worked. She would beam at us and say "yes!"

This went on for some time and it increased our faith and obviously helped her to fit in and feel comfortable.

Then we heard the story of her tragedy. It was of huge proportion and had caused a severe breakdown in her capacity to relate and to be coherent. We all prayed for her healing. And it came. Not instantly, not rapidly, in fact it came almost undiscerned, as it was inch by inch over months. But it was complete and she was completely understandable after that.

I THINK WE SHOULD
TAKE A DOG

Our friends had this wonderful holiday home in a valley about four hours north of Cape Town; remote, unspoiled, and spectacularly beautiful, and we were going there for a break. We packed all the sorts of things one needs, old clothes, swim suits, easy to cook food. We'd been before so we knew what was necessary.

Then Grace said 'I think we should take a dog'. After all these years I didn't ask her why, and so we borrowed a Jack Russell who seemed absolutely thrilled about it.

It was as beautiful as we remembered, and the road into the area was awful and almost non-negotiable as well. We walked, climbed, swam, and read from the large supply of books packing the bookcases on the walls of the main room. We looked at the stars that seemed so close one could try and touch them, managed the odd braai (barbecue) and enjoyed the unspoiledness, the quietness, and the space.

On the third day we decided to walk through the orchard to the waterfall behind the house, a morning's trip. We crossed the stream on a wonderful rope and plank bridge and set out for the mountain, with Tatu, the dog, exploring everything ahead of us.

Thank goodness she was ahead of us, for suddenly she froze, as a huge cobra rose from the path and towered over her. She was about 10–15 metres away. I stopped dead in my tracks, and Grace crashed into me. She began to ask what was wrong, and then she saw, and started to pray.

"Tatu", I screamed, and she turned, ran flat out and landed in my arms with an exhibition of obedience that was unusual for her. I somewhat regretted my shout when she started shaking violently – I remembered being told that one needed to be absolutely still in confrontations with snakes – and there was no way Tatu was able to fulfil that requirement. I covered her up as far as I could with my arms and wondered what on earth to do next.

I looked at the snake and it looked at me. It was huge; its head seemed about the same height as mine, about the size of my spread out hand, and its body as thick as my arm. Irrelevantly I wondered, if it should bite me, what possible good a tourniquet around my neck would be. The absurdity of that thought brought me back to reality, and I started to think more helpfully.

"Grace," I said quietly, "Start walking backwards very slowly, and put out a hand so I don't step back into you, and you can keep me steady." As if there were any hope of me being steady when I was frankly terrified, and Tatu with me.

Small step by small step we retreated. It seemed like forever, but finally we were about a hundred yards away. This seemed to satisfy the cobra, who put down its hood and lowered itself into the grass.

Actually that was unnerving, as then we couldn't locate it, so we turned around and got to the bridge as fast as we could.

We didn't go along that path again.

We wondered what would have happened if we had not had a dog running around in front of us that morning.

I thanked God yet again for a friend who heard Him, so often and so helpfully.

ADRIAN AND ROS
AND THE KAROO

We met Adrian and Ros because the bishop of Port Elizabeth, the same Bruce who had been rector of St John's Wynberg, told us to go and spend time with them. There was a 'move of the Spirit' in the area, Bruce said, and Adrian was the most amazing evangelist, but could not cope with the greatly increased numbers of folk coming to him and his widely scattered churches. He found that he wasn't sure how to cope with this added dimension. "Please go and give him whatever help he needs" were our instructions. And so we went, and hoped we would manage the rest. That is how we met one of the most wonderful couples in all our time in South Africa.

It was a long way, a full day's journey right into the heartland of the Karoo, a great arid semi-desert area in the middle of the country. The name Karoo was apparently a bushman name and means 'the great thirst'. We discovered over the years just how apt the name was. But the dryness meant one could see forever, and the colors are beyond description. It is one of the most beautiful and awesome places on the planet.

We arrived, and were greeted by Adrian's wonderful grin and Ros' never failing welcome, and a lasting friendship began. It was tough going though, with endless travel. Adrian, Grace and I would leave early in the morning to head for some distant farmhouse or 'dorp' (a local term for small hamlet), anything up to four hours non-stop travel. We never seemed to have a set program but rather went along with what Adrian and our hosts preferred. Sometimes we went straight into a group of folk who were full of questions, other times they simply waited to see what we were offering first. All wanted to have a more positive effect through their faith, so we were pretty much on the same page.

We talked together about the importance Jesus put on the effect on His followers of the Holy Spirit's coming, and explored together what this might look like, and where they could find the relevant information in their Bibles. Often the discussion and questions went on far longer than the allotted time, and we either kept going into the night, or came back when we could. It was hugely rewarding, and worth the almost permanent tiredness.

And the stories slowly built up. There was a farmer who thought to ask why so many of his men were living with women they were not married to. The answer was simple. They could not afford a wedding. He decided to solve it. He organized a mass wedding, paid for the reception, and then sent them all off to a nearby holiday resort to have a short honeymoon.

A police sergeant asked a farmer what was new. The farmer thought for a few minutes, and then said that the answer might be the Holy Spirit, although he wasn't sure one could call the Holy Spirit new. "That would explain my problem," replied the sergeant. "I haven't had a crime reported in months." I guess I should not have been as surprised as I was, for that is, after all, what is supposed to happen.

We spent nights or weekends staying with families, and got to know many quite well, and it was a wonderfully rewarding time. The one thing I wish I could have changed though was the setting sun in our faces as we drove back to Cape Town.

We went to the Karoo regularly for the next ten years spending about a month each year, and every visit was wonderful. Then Adrian and Ros moved from Middleburg, and we moved up to Johannesburg, and our special visits ended.

But there was a lovely incident a long time later. Grace, our friend Jane (more about her later), and I had been to Cape Town and were making the long drive back to Johannesburg. On a whim we decided to stay in Colesberg. It is a little over half way and a lovely spot. We had stayed there or around the area many times with Adrian, and it felt good to do so again. We chose to stay at the accommodation offered by the pub, as they were renowned for serving the best lamb shank we had ever tasted. When we went in for dinner we started to chat to the friendly, but very busy, lady in charge. She asked us if we had been in the area before and we said yes and started to name a few people we had known quite well. Suddenly she interrupted us and said, "You must be Grace and Helen!" We admitted we were. Then she told us her story. Her parents had found faith during one of our visits around thirty years before. Their children, of whom she was one, had all come to faith, and all her children as well, as they all wanted the same assurance and answers.

It was one of those amazing moments that leave one breathless. So often we only heard the problems and never got to find out any long-term answers.

The lamb was as good as we remembered, and she found time to come and chat with us and catch us up with all the local news.

MONEY FOR THE RENT

In Cape Town we found a permanent home. Before that we had lived in our car and a tent as mostly we were travelling all over the country. It was a very nice second floor flat overlooking Rhodes' Memorial and Table mountain, and had been found by a couple of new friends who went hunting for us. It was cheap and accessible and we loved it. But, it was getting towards the end of the month and we were short of money. We needed R80 to pay the rent and we did not have a tenth of that. Grace suggested I search my pockets, normally that would have yielded something, but, alas, they were empty.

We prayed that someone would be prompted to give to us, and they did. The day before the rent was due we opened the door to the loveliest bouquet of flowers delivered by a rather smart florist. The gift was anonymous and brightened us with its beauty. Someone had been very generous. Only ... it was hard to see how it helped our dilemma. I rather dryly asked Grace whether any of the flowers were edible and we both started laughing. It was lovely, and we enjoyed it, but were no nearer having the cash to pay the rent.

"What now?" I asked Grace, who replied, "We can always try buttons," laughed, and suggested we went for a walk, which we did. It seemed a suitable diversion from the problem of the rent. We walked up to the Memorial, watched the wildebeest as they frolicked without care, and did our best to follow their example as we returned home.

When we went into the sitting room we noticed two envelopes that had appeared on the table against the wall. One said 'Grace,' and the other 'Helen.' We opened them. Inside each was R80 in nice clean notes

To this day we have no human explanation for those envelopes. No one knew we needed the money. No one had access to our flat. And the table was against an inside wall. I almost hesitate to include this incident as it really does defy any explanation I can come up with.

Except, God heard and answered our prayer.

By the way, it goes alongside finding Swiss francs by the side of the road, being given Yugoslav money by a man who we saw pushing his car and guessed rightly that he would like some of the petrol we carried to get him to the next garage, and being brought orange juice when suffering from a bad bought of dysentery in Kabul.

All needs we could not meet ourselves that turned into encouragements to keep us going.

DON'T WORRY, THERE IS AN ANGEL

We had a dear friend who lived at the other end of the Republic. We had known each other for years, and would have lunch together if we found ourselves in the same town – we used to chat over the phone a couple of times a month.

One day she phoned us from Durban (we were standing in a car park in Cape Town hundreds of miles away.) "I need help," she said. "Robert, (her unstable son, who caused her much grief), has come home. He is in one of his rages and says he is going to kill me. He has gone to get his gun."

We felt helpless, so far away, and prayed that wonderful prayer, "Help!" And the answer came instantly, which of course was what she had phoned for. "Don't worry, there is an angel between you and him." We got no further, for she exclaimed, "He is coming back." And the phone went dead. We prayed as hard as we knew how, standing in that dark and busy car park, for we understood how real the threat was.

About two minutes later, it felt like forever, the phone rang again. "It's me," she said "He came in, pointed the gun at my stomach and fired it. The bullet dropped to the floor in front of me. We looked at it and then at each other, and then the gun. He pointed it at the ceiling and fired it. The bullet went through the ceiling and the roof and he has run out screaming.

I know the feathers of the angel protected me."

Isn't that wonderful! Indeed it was. It really was.

We went into the mall and had a strong coffee and wondered at the miracle that had happened, and did our best to get over the shock of it all.

Our friend had to get the house repaired, and she was never again paralyzed by fear of Robert.

DID ANYONE HEAR
WHAT HE SAID?

We were deep in the heartland of tough farming country, where it was very hard to make a living, where a lot of the conflicts of history were just below the surface, where folk struggled with life and how to survive, where talking about what one felt was simply not done. Not the easiest place to be invited to.

We were speaking at a meeting put together by local Christians who hoped against hope that something we said might offer a glimmer of hope? I think they knew not what – just that they were desperate enough to try anything. I admired their courage, for the crowd assembled looked like rough, tough farmers and wives who were not often caught attending a meeting in a church hall on a Saturday afternoon, and I was glad that it was Grace who was speaking.

She spoke in that whimsical, utterly convincing way she has, on how it was possible to hear God. That He was always trying to get through to us and, just as every human had learned to listen and understand from their parents – or those who fulfilled the role – so we could with God.

She gave wonderfully simple and real examples to illustrate it all.

Then she talked about how we could hear such different things within the same incident. She used a bit in John's gospel,

(12:28–9) where Jesus was praying and His Father replied to Him. It says, "The crowd that was there heard it, they said that it had thundered; others said an angel had spoken to Him."

As she said that, there was a deafening clap of thunder out of a clear blue sky. The silence following was long, very long. Finally one of the men said, "Did anyone hear what He said?" We all started to laugh, out of sheer relief that the tension was broken, but the point was made.

We broke for tea shortly thereafter. What more could anyone say after that? But the reality seemed to be accepted and the atmosphere became far more relaxed. We found ourselves able to discuss things and explore possible ways forward, and we were even asked to come back next time we were in the area.

OUR FIRST VISIT
TO HONG KONG

It was 1985, and we were nearly at the end of our time in Cape Town. We had been there for a little over ten years. Initially we had spent most of our time moving all over the country trying, in the words of the then Archbishop of Cape Town, to bring Good News to folk rather than good advice. We had seen the excitement of the move of the Spirit across the spectrum of the church, and we had seen the gradual return to the status quo in many places.

For the last two years we had been leading a church in Wynberg where there were wonderful folk, and we enjoyed them greatly. But the endless red tape and historical and pointless restrictions stopped so much of what could and should have happened. We were also confronted, almost daily, with the issues, pain and anger caused by the Apartheid situation, and felt trapped between a rock and a hard place as the old saying goes.

Every monday we, as part of a leadership of a large parish, met for the morning. It was usually pretty predictable, looking at what had happened in the previous week, what might in the next one, and general discussion about the situation in the country.

This particular week we had a visitor, someone from Hong Kong called Jackie Pullinger. She was visiting her friend from school days, who was the wife of the rector. I don't remember much about that morning or of her. She was briefly introduced. What she was doing in Hong Kong was sketchedly covered, really so briefly that it made little impression on me, though it sounded a lot more interesting than what most people did.

We got on with the morning meeting.

At lunch time she asked me if I would like to go to Hong Kong to visit her. I said "Yes." Later Grace came to me laughing. She said Jackie had repeated our conversation to her and asked what "Yes" meant. Clearly it had been a bit brief as an answer. Grace said that, if I said yes I meant just that. She said Jackie seemed relieved. Grace had also been asked, and gave a fuller reply. So, maybe we would go sometime …

Jackie had been asked to speak all over the area while she was in Wynberg, and we were designated as the ones who got her there and back again. We were delighted. We spent most of the next few days doing this, and as the meetings went on for hours – for folk wanted everything there was for them – this meant we seldom dropped her off at the Rectory before midnight.

One evening we asked Jackie if, rather than going straight back, she would prefer to go somewhere where we could have a drink and something to eat. Her eyes lit up and off we went.

Sometimes so much seems to have come from the smallest decision. We had time to talk, to ask and answer questions, and to discover that we were on the same page concerning many things. I could not wait to get to Hong Kong and see for myself the life she so tantalisingly talked about.

It also confirmed the feeling we had had that it was time we moved on, so we left our jobs and Cape Town after Christmas, packed our stuff in the car and drove to Johannesburg. We stayed with friends for a couple of exhausted days and then flew East.

It was magic seeing the islands of the South China Sea spread out below us, and the fairytale skyscrapers on the island. We flew frighteningly low over the Walled City, dropped onto the only-just-long-enough runway in Kowloon, and were delighted to find ourselves safely stationary before we went into the sea.

Even more wonderful was to find ourselves staying in Hang Fook Camp, a refugee camp that had just been handed over to Jackie as accommodation for the large number of folk who had come off drugs. Here they found an alternative to belonging to Triad gangs, had been rescued from the streets, and were all trying to live out their new faith in Jesus with the help of young helpers from all over the world who, like us, had met Jackie and accepted her invitation to 'come, see.'

I loved it. From day one I loved it. It contained not much that was appealing humanly, yet everything that I had always longed to be part of. I saw the good news reaching everyone who wanted it, regardless of where they were or how they were. I saw the gospel in all its simple and compelling power reaching the manifestly lost and transforming the found. It was the reality of radical change and the love of God let loose. What more could I want or dream of. I felt as though I had come home.

From the beginning we got involved. We stayed, as I said, in this refugee camp, a tiny series of huts surrounded by multi-storied buildings. 'Basic' would be a good word to describe it. It had water (cold), and loo's with plastic sheeting doors, and tin tables and no extras. It also had a togetherness and a sense of God about to do something that was stunning.

Every Sunday we were filled to overflowing with individuals coming to the Sunday afternoon service, which was full of enthusiastic singing, lots of stories, and a wonderful sense of things about to happen ... which they did. Brother after brother stood up and told the story about his struggle to come off drugs and how he was still free from them, how he had prayed for someone and they were healed, or "And this is my brother/family/mother who I am reunited with". The biggest cheer was likely to be the new brother or sister who had just left the addict scene and was now walking with Jesus. It was all just such fun.

But we became really part of that later, as Jackie had other ideas about our usefulness. We had only been there a few days when she sent us off to start a new house on Laama Island. "Lame Island?" I exclaimed as she calmly unfolded her plan. "Where in the world is that?" It turned out that it was Lamma, not Lame, and we would go to the drug addict's meeting held in the Walled City every Thursday, and afterwards go with Ah Yin, (soon to become a lifelong friend), and another two brothers and two addicts to a flat on the Island. She made it sound so matter of fact and easy. I think my doubts about the venture were perhaps nearer the mark.

We went to the walled city meeting. It was breathtaking to see so many, mostly young people, crammed into the room in the middle of this notorious place, absolutely lost in the wonder of answers instead of hopeless despair. Not that we understood a word of it. Actually, that was me, as Grace, with that uncanny way she has with languages, was already accumulating useful words of Cantonese. We went to the harbour with our helpers and our addicts still high on drugs. We made the trip to Lamma Island, arriving long after dark, walked down a track that one of the old brothers seemed to know, found our destination in spite of everything and proceeded to 'set up a new boy house' as instructed, but probably not quite as anticipated by those who sent us.

We spent most of the rest of the night half watching to see that our precious new, still high on heroin, brothers were safe, and partly looking at the strange junks and fishing boats in the Bay.

Of course it was diving in at the deep end, and we sometimes felt we were drowning. But we did not. We learned the ropes. We stayed there for six weeks, hopefully getting better at the job, and then went back to Hang Fook camp. It was awful, and yet all of us who were a part of making it home, all look back on that time there with longing.

We have been to help in Hong Kong again and again in the intervening twenty-five years, and every time has been that refreshing challenge and blessing that the first time was. It seems a second home.

AND THEN JOHANNESBURG

When we returned from Hong Kong we settled in Johannesburg.

The last thing we had done after leaving Cape Town before flying out was to drive up there, leave our car with our dear friends Ronnie and Nan, and take a deep breath, for we knew one part of our journey was over, and that Jo'burg would be very different. The degree to which it was we had not guessed. Johannesburg is a long way north of Cape Town where we had been based. It is also very different.

It was a huge and rapidly growing city. No Table Mountain to tell you where you were when you got lost, any number of suburbs and communities, more 'townships,' and nearby towns. The pace was quicker, the unrest more tangible, and the risks more evident. It was much more difficult to find our way around, definitely more dangerous, and we had to get better at map reading and estimating the time it would take us to get to places we had to speak at.

We had to get used to a lot of new realities.

The first thing we did was to look for a flat, which turned out to be very easy and within short walking distance from Ron and Nan. It had space, was well placed for travelling, and surprisingly cheap. We were delighted.

The second was to talk with the clergyman who had suggested we come and work with him. He was doing amazing things, but it was clear that we would not fit easily into his plans or vision, and we all had the wisdom to accept that and part as friends.

What to do instead was not a problem. Very quickly we found we were getting invitations from all over the Transvaal (now called Gauteng), the province Johannesburg is in, as well as the country at large. In fact there was hardly anywhere we didn't go as the requests came pouring in. I think we were asked so often because we offered good news rather than un-doable advice. Or, perhaps, we were simply the flavour of the month. We became ever more adept at coping with constant change, and meeting yet another group of people we did not know. We even got to know the geography of the North, and which routes to take, and which to avoid.

Above everything, we had to stay flexible. One week we would be with church groups in Johannesburg and the next travelling west to a Catholic cathedral of great beauty with a sense of God's presence that was rare. From there to the south of Natal (now KwaZuluNatal), or Bophuthatswana (now North West), hundreds of miles apart. We learned first hand just how big South Africa was – and how far apart the petrol stations were at times! We also learned how to deal with the increasing number of road blocks, the signs of unrest, fires burning all over the place, and to listen to folk in the garages where we filled up as they would tell us if we should avoid a particular route.

Who did we visit? Some of the groups consisted of a few friends who wanted input and encouragement; some were established congregations who were specific about their needs and desires. The common denominator was desperation to find a faith and answers that would help in the increasingly precarious and violent situation we all lived in. So a faith that could help in the situation was very much the order of the day. We basically accepted every invitation we could. And did the best we could each time. I doubt we did the same twice because no two groups were the same.

Most often, but by no means exclusively, we were invited by those who wanted to know more about the Holy Spirit, and how they might function with His gifts and power. Jesus was very clear that it was through the coming of the Holy Spirit that His followers would find the power they needed to live out their faith in the precarious and often hostile environment of the Roman Empire. We saw that the Spirit's presence made such a difference to His followers all those centuries ago, and also among the people we met week after week.

As things got worse, and the violence and protest more intense, the clampdown by the authorities increased everywhere, especially in Soweto and the Vaal triangle. Armored vehicles, soldiers and endless clashes were daily news. We saw them and heard the gunshots and were stopped at roadblocks as we continued to travel wherever we were asked to.

Some events still stand out clearly. I can remember driving from White River in the North East, just below the Kruger Park, back to Johannesburg. We went through road blocks all the way, fires, protests, demonstrations, and a profound sense of the need for answers to what looked like unanswerable anger on one side, and stubborn holding out on the other, with a lot of loss on both sides. It was a long and traumatic journey. It seemed as night fell that the whole country was on fire.

Yet it was a wonderful time in some ways as we all hung together. We lived in that state all the time, and I think I finally understood my mother's comments about her life during the Second World War. She had a young family, her husband was in the Army, and she coped, as everyone else did, it seemed, by hanging in together. She remained wistfully appreciative of those times as her circle shrunk and she was often lonely. Whatever the dangers and trauma of the war had been, she had never been lonely.

From our move there in 1985 until the New South Africa emerged in 1997, this is how we lived most of the time. Always somewhere doing something. A lot of it has got blurred as time passes, but the odd thing stands out in my memory. I think it was the determination to find a way through by all but the diehard right wing that won the day. And the example of so many doing the small something that they could. The huge risks, courage and cost that those on the cutting edge endured made many of us keep on trying, however useless our situation looked. For despair walked alongside even the most hopeful, as people were persecuted, imprisoned, disappeared, protested, tried to find ways of surviving in the prolonged death throes of Apartheid. Fear was a constant reality.

It helped enormously when FW de Klerk came to power. Perhaps it was the slight lightening of darkness that precluded the dawn of a new day however distant. At least there was movement, and finally Nelson Mandela walked free, the elections happened, and the African National Congress came into power.

PSALM 46:1

We were in Port Elizabeth, a major port on the east coast of South Africa. We were speaking at the first joint meeting of the Anglican ladies group and the Methodist ladies group. It was certainly an important day, especially at that time, the mid 1970's, when things were tending to fragment rather than come together, and it was great that these two women's groups had bridged the gap. This is a mild way of saying that indignation and anger over apartheid and its injustices were everywhere, tension really did fill the air, and it was incredibly brave for them to be coming together in this way.

After the preliminaries, Grace was invited to speak. She stood up and quoted Psalm 46:1 – "God is our refuge and strength, a very present help in trouble." Then she went on to tell them how God had been to her a 'refuge and strength, a very present help in times of trouble,' in her tumultuous days in Eritrea in the 1960's.

She spoke of riots and violence, of 'rebels' being hung on the lampposts of the streets while the population was forced to watch them die. Of students targeting schools and how the school that she was in charge of (in her 20's) was the only one they had not trashed, although they had got as far as the end of the road. She told of seeing God protect the children and people in the community, and what she and her teachers and pupils had done and prayed as the anger against the regime of the Emperor spilled out on the streets. Apparently ordinary people found healing and faith, and saw miracles day by day, as they put their faith into action. It was wonderful stuff.

Then she stopped.

A long silence followed. Unusually long, it seemed to last forever. Finally the leader stood up. She was a woman of great presence, and everyone waited in the silence. She seemed to be struggling to speak. Then she began.

"My sisters," she said with desperate intensity, "Before today, I would have said, when the trouble came, the whites have given us a faith of many words but no answers. Nothing to meet our needs in what is coming upon us, nothing that will help us care for our children, our families, our neighbors." She paused and the silence was total.

Then she went on to say, "But, she said … and we will do …" she said … and we will do …" She went through the whole of Grace's input, point-by-point saying, "She said, or did this … And we shall do this. She said that … and we will do this." She spoke of all sorts of situations, and applied Grace's experiences and wisdom to them. One by one. It was a wonderful taking of what was said and applying it to some future possibility. Every one was listening with the same intensity that the leader was speaking with. It was hard to remember to breathe.

Grace and I sat there realizing something very important was happening. But we didn't know what. For although the whole area was full of tension, protests and outbreaks of violence, what we had found was not more than we expected. And there had been no violent incidents that day as far as we knew. Yet, we caught the tension and the involvement, and the way every word the leader spoke was being responded to.

She stopped.

There was yet another long silence. It seemed as though the many women there started to breathe again. The leader turned to Grace and said, "I thank you my sister. You have given us the answers we need."

Then she hugged her. And me. And everyone started to hug each other and talk non-stop.

The meeting broke up after a while, and the women started to talk to each other in Xhosa. We went home very grateful for how helpful Gracie seemed to have been, warmed by their warmth, but with no real answers as to what had taken place, or why the reaction had been what it was.

We got some answers as we left the city early the next day to drive hundreds of miles North West back to Johannesburg.

The townships were ablaze, burning tires were sending their black acrid fumes to the protesting skies, and mayhem, road blocks, police and army tanks and danger were everywhere.

We had not known, as those women had known, that the impending explosion we were all waiting for was scheduled for the very next day. Nor that what Grace had shared was so imminently needed by those dear brave women.

USELESS WATER

We were in a country area in a beautiful and flourishing town, visiting a lovely church full of people who were doing their best to make a positive difference to their community and those in need. They were such great people who were doing very good stuff. But they were getting tired, and finding it hard to keep going.

"Do something" said their Rector. Not an easy request to satisfy. Actually it felt more like a mixture of a sob of despair and an imperative, for he had given everything he had and was not seeing the breakthrough they needed. He was quite right in his diagnosis; they were definitely running out of steam.

Yet they were also a community who had known something of the Holy Spirit coming to them. And that gave us the clue we needed concerning the answer. The Book talks about followers of Jesus receiving the Holy Spirit and impacting the community, and then it talks of them getting tired, and needing more. At least this had happened before. It certainly fitted the situation.

I was supposed to talk at the morning service, so I spent time talking through the problem with the Almighty. He gave me a verse from the gospel of John, "If anyone is thirsty, let him come to me and drink. Out of him will flow rivers of living water."

It seemed a starting point, but even so I was not that confident, so I prayed hard for inspiration. I understood how irritating it can be when one is tired, when someone offers advice, which seems, frankly, unhelpful.

Come the service I simply got more nervous and asked more desperately for inspiration. A thought came into my mind, and I hoped it was the missing thing. When it was time to speak I stood in the pulpit, picked up the glass of water, which is always at hand for needy preachers, and said "I am thirsty". They looked at me without comment. I said it again, still clutching the glass of water. "I am thirsty, what can I do?" No one answered me. I tried again. "What can I do to satisfy my thirst?" No response. In despair I poured the entire glass over myself and said, "I am still thirsty." That got their attention.

I pointed out that I had had the answer to my need, but was not using it to meet that need. There was no point in holding a glass of water in my hand and saying I was thirsty when all I needed to do was drink it. And there was absolutely no point doing anything else with the provision of my needs except the obvious, as my wet clothes demonstrated. Nothing but getting it inside us and seeing the benefits happen will do.

Then we looked again at the Book. At how the early Christians seemed to have had the same problems we do. It's hard to keep on keeping on. It is hard to keep receiving when we want it just to be there permanently. The sheer normality and obviousness of it all turned out to be very reassuring to many, and helped get the community going again. They continued to be an answer to many of the needs in their community. They also had the answer for themselves.

I have yet to forget it for myself.

ANOTHER UNLIKELY ANSWER

In the same province but a very different situation:

Caroline was a name from the past. She had met Grace when they were attending the same course at YWAM in Switzerland. She was a Zulu from Zululand, and she had heard that Grace was now in South Africa and asked her to speak at a ladies conference she was organizing. It was for leaders from quite an extensive area, and was to be held in a place right down in the southern tip of Zululand. Because I now worked with Grace, I was invited as well.

We had moved to Johannesburg by that time, and it was a very long journey – mostly on roads we didn't know – so we set off before dawn. It was in the country, and it really was as far south as Zululand went, in a very rural place, miles it seemed, from anywhere. The quality of the roads deteriorated the further we got, but it was rather fun to be right in the countryside. That was, as long as we made it in time ... which we did, all of half an hour before the program was scheduled to start.

We were the only speakers, and the only ones from outside Zululand, and we got caught up in the exuberance; the whole-hearted way everything was done, and the beauty of the singing. It was heartwarming, different, and long. Everyone took part in everything. There was no holding back. Whatever was on offer they went for, particularly when prayer was available.

Given the needs, that was inevitable, as there were so many things individuals wanted that they could see only God could meet.

These sessions were not quiet. Many expressed their feelings, pain and desires out loud, sometimes, very loud.

I found it a refreshing alternative to the withdrawn response of so many other groups I had been with. Grace and I quickly became fully involved in it all.

Then, I saw her. A lady at the back who looked as though she was about to explode. Some pent up experience or problem was going to have to find a way out, and it was going to pretty quickly by the look of it. Grace was thoroughly involved with what was happening at the front, so I promptly left the platform and headed for the lady at the back. It was not easy to get to her as I had to get past a lot of ladies who were entirely involved with their own stuff, and I had to squeeze past folk when there really was not space to do so. Just before I reached her she let out the most ear-shattering shriek I think I have ever heard, and fell to the floor. I had been around long enough to know that the widely held belief in the presence of demons was well justified.

The Bible makes it quite clear that this is a normal part of life so it didn't worry me. What I wanted to avoid was what seemed the rough way it was sometimes dealt with, especially in communities who recognized the reality and were determined to see their friends freed. I had seen what looked to me like pretty strong stuff, a whole group getting involved, surrounding and shaking the person, shouting, getting into a bit of a state themselves, a lot of noise, and much emotion. I had also seen enough already in the meeting to suspect it would happen again if I could not show a gentler way that was also effective.

So, I tried it. I simply talked to her quietly, about how much

God loved her, and how Jesus was bigger and stronger than any demon. I repeated the message that God loved her and was going to rescue her and set her free and this seemed to help her the most. Gradually the lady seemed to be responding.

Of course, by this time no one was facing the front. Everyone present had swung round at the shriek. I talked about Jesus being angry at the demons not the victims, and continued this double conversation, to the lady getting free, and the women listening intently. Gradually the lady stopped screaming and a peace came. We talked quietly together for a short time, and then, as she was restored to normal, she took her seat again and I leant against the back wall in relief.

Afterwards we all had a long discussion about what had happened, and the ladies were quite taken with the quieter approach I had used. It actually transformed the weekend, as we were able to interact more and speak less. We chatted and discussed and most of the ladies wanted to be prayed for, and we became a happy bunch together with the gulf between speaker and audience non-existent.

THE SNAKE

We were staying in Ulundi, the capital of Natal, at the invitation of the rector of the church, Rev Siphu Miandu. He was the most wonderful carer of his people, and we loved our time with him.

Every afternoon, except Sunday when we spent the day at the church, we headed for the villages on the hills, which were of some considerable distance and height, and well off the beaten track. It was always clear afternoon daylight when we left Ulundi and dusk or dark when we got to our destination.

On arrival we would find ourselves in a kraal with traditional round mud and thatch huts. We would be met by the wonderful sound and sight of singing and dancing, and be part of that until we were asked to contribute. We did our best to speak of things that would meet needs, fortunately having been given enough clues by Siphu to have some idea where to start.

The light came from torches, which cast huge and moving shadows everywhere. There was a space for us to stand, sometimes in a building but usually under a large thatched roof with no walls. With the flickering light from torches placed strategically around and the involvement of everyone in what was happening, they were wonderful evenings.

Afterwards, and that was always deep into the night, we would climb back into the car and make the long and winding trip home.

I remember these nights with delight for they were wonderful, and we were allowed to be a real part of it all. As the evening went on, the differences between us visitors and locals seemed to disappear. We shared the good news, and individuals experienced God meeting them where they wanted or needed.

But, one night remains vividly in my mind.

This particular village was further away from Ulundi than the others and quite an effort to get to with endless switchbacks and narrow bits on the road. The village seemed larger and the numbers greater. We were met by a lot of people who thronged around us. For reasons we didn't understand there was tension in the air and it was an effort to stay calm. We were steered into one end of a huge space covered by a circular thatched roof. I thought it was probably the local equivalent of the village hall I had known in Surrey. As we moved towards it Grace and I were both aware of an unstated problem. Something in the atmosphere alerted us to we-knew-not-what, but it was tangible.

We were put in the middle of the hut so we had a semicircle of people around us, and a large number outside. They could see, as the hut did not have walls, only poles holding the roof up.

I stood behind Grace, and could not see very much because she was taller than I am. It was so full there was simply no free space. Grace started to speak and quickly captured the attention of the crowd. Siphu interpreted, and the audience seemed engrossed in the things Grace was telling them.

The flickering light, moving shadows and the strangeness of it all began to seem normal and rather fascinating, and we were all part of the wonder of the old story. I relaxed, as I thought whatever had been the problem seemed to have gone. I was wrong. Grace suddenly came to an abrupt halt and said,

"Help!" in the most desperate tone. I was behind her standing on a small platform so I could not really see much. "What is wrong?" I asked in the calmest tone I could manage – it had to be bad if Grace panicked. "This lady has just writhed through everyone up to me, reared up like a snake, and I am afraid she is going to bite me. She's like a snake."

I said the first thing that came into my head. (which probably was from God) "Tell her to go away." So she did. "Go away in the name of Jesus". The most awful terrifying screaming started. It seemed to come from hell. I held my breath. I suspect we all did.

Then the strangest, or most wonderful thing happened. The screaming stopped. It was replaced by shouting and singing and dancing and rejoicing, which to me was as unexpected and un-understandable as the snake and the screaming had been. Apparently the lady in question had seemed to deflate and writhe away.

The entire company present, with the exception of Grace and myself, seemed to be having a celebration. Definitely preferable to what had gone on before. But why … and what in the world (or out of it) had been going on? After a time things quieted enough for the local chief to give us the answer. The lady/snake was a very powerful Sangoma who held the community in fear. She was not someone who used her powers to try and help as so many Sangoma's do. She used them to get her own way.

The conversation went on, and on, as the villagers asked us to tell them more. So we spoke of the One who was stronger than any other, and who brought life and freedom and the ability to defeat the powers of darkness. They listened with intensity. Siphu arranged to come back and tell them more so they could live in a new freedom.

We danced and hugged each other and left.

When we got to the car we found, as so often happened, a deep fog had cut visibility dramatically, and so we crawled down the hill at snail's pace until we got below the cloud. It took a long time to get home.

But it didn't matter. God had come in that place.

UNEXPECTED INPUT

Grace and I had been running a monthly ladies meeting in a church Hall in Rosebank for quite a long time. They were fun, and seemed to be worth attending for the hall was usually quite full. Some people we knew fairly well, some became close friends, and some we simply enjoyed without invading their privacy at all. We often started with music or singing, and always had a break where we could just chat. There was input and response, and then we all went our different ways.

We never knew quite what would happen at any time. It depended on who came, whether folk wanted a lot of discussion or individual time, it was pretty flexible, and we enjoyed it. But, sometimes we were surprised by what happened.

I particularly remember one session. This was when Grace spoke to a lady we had begun to know. She was middle aged, came regularly and we enjoyed her quiet presence. That particular week Grace went to her and said, "I really think you should go and see a doctor, today." The lady looked at her in amazement and protested that there was nothing wrong with her, she didn't feel ill, so why should she go? Grace simply said that she felt strongly she should go, and not delay but to go that afternoon.

The lady smiled, and left. We did not see her for weeks, and having no address or telephone number we couldn't contact her.

About four months later she returned. Shyly she approached Grace and told her the story. She had been shocked by what Grace had said, but impressed by the calm yet insistent way Grace had spoken to her. "It can't do me any harm to go", she thought so she made the appointment and went, that afternoon.

The doctor had examined her and said she was on the brink of having a heart attack, and had her admitted to hospital that afternoon. She had the needed heart surgery. The doctor said she would not have survived long without the surgical intervention. She was really lucky as the lack of symptoms could have been fatal.

We were awed. So pleased that Grace had heard God when it really mattered, and that the lady had gone to the doctor when she could so easily have ignored Grace's words.

Another unexpected input was directed at me, at the same monthly meeting, though on a different day. I was starting things off that morning and had been standing behind the microphone waiting for everyone to arrive and get seated. A woman who was sitting in the front row suddenly got up, came in front of me and said, very emotionally, "I hate you. I hate everything about you. But it is not personal." She just stood glaring at me. I thought, "I can accept that she may hate me. I can even accept that she may hate everything about me. But why, I wondered, was that not personal?" Before I could say anything, though I had no idea at all about what I might say, the lady glared at me once more, returned to her seat on the front row, and continued to stare daggers at me.

It was not by any stretch of the imagination an easy start. I prayed that wonderful prayer "Help!" and somehow got started, managed to keep going, and came to a relieved end without losing track of what I was saying.

Our break for tea was so very welcome, as at least I didn't have to cope with the lady emitting fury at me. As I drank my tea I asked the Almighty what, if anything, I should do. Then I went to her and said, "I can understand that you might hate me. I can understand that you might hate everything about me. What I don't understand is why it is not personal." She folded in front of me, flung her arms around me and sobbed and sobbed. Finally, as the pent up pain was released she muttered, "You remind me of my mother." From there, and with help from one or two helpful folk she received some long needed healing and left relatively happily.

I didn't see her again. Perhaps she was embarrassed to come back; perhaps she only needed to come once. But I have thought of her down the years, and was so grateful that I was given the help I needed to deal with her gently.

AND THEN THERE
WERE CONFERENCES

Of course there were. It seems that they are a part of life. And certainly a part of the life of the church in South Africa. I am putting it in here because it probably needs to appear somewhere, but really it is a minor part of life and not a favorite one.

The first one we took an active part in was being put together by an eclectic group of folk who saw the desire of many to learn about the Holy Spirit, and decided to do something about it.

It was called the Cape Town Renewal Conference and was held at the Cape Town Civic Centre in 1981, and, as I look back, was one of the best we were part of. I think that was because we were from so many and varied backgrounds and churches, all seeing it as something we wanted to be part of and so we happily got stuck in it together.

Archbishop Bill Burnett led from the front with all his enthusiasm and commitment; Dave and Dale Garret brought singing and worship such as many of us had not known before. Derek Prince spoke with a clarity and relevance that caught our commitment and helped many move forward in their faith. Terry Fullam, a jovial Anglican from Darien, captivated us with wonderful singing and his choice of songs. The graphic way he explained the Bible made one want to read it again and again. We all thought he was perhaps the best Bible teacher we were ever likely to encounter

It was the happiest of all the conferences I have attended because it seemed, at least for then, as though we were what we were supposed to be, one happy family.

We ran a number of smaller events and also went to one in Singapore for Anglicans from all over the world. At one point we all got divided into small groups, and then were sent all over the place. Grace and I found ourselves in Sri Lanka. It was fascinating, and the strangest things stick in my memory:

- That our hosts were so disappointed that we were white skinned.
- That the mosquito nets around our beds seemed to be very good at keeping the mosquitos in, and we were both quickly covered with bites that seemed to be at least four times as big as the ones we got at home.
- That everywhere we went, women who had endless questions surrounded us. They didn't want to leave until they got the answers they needed. I don't know that I have ever faced a more desperate desire for help.

Then there was Nancy Honeytree. One of the original Jesus people from the USA, she was full of stories of those carefree days, sang wonderful songs, most of which she had written, and could get almost everyone singing them within seconds. She won our hearts, with her deep and simple faith, her transparent nature, and the fun she exuded. She had a crazy sense of humor, and we enjoyed her times with us very much. She was also refreshingly honest about how difficult it could all be.

Some years later we went with her to India. We started off in a city with all the expected amenities of a city, and were the only ones from South Africa. Most were from the USA or Mexico, where the leader of the group lived. It was interesting, fascinating, and we learned all sorts of other ways of doing things.

Our team was asked to introduce themselves. Each of us was allotted two minutes. But the first two to go took twenty-five between them, so it seemed a good idea to be very brief. I simply said, "I'm Helen, I come from South Africa, I am single, and I love it". Hardly memorable I thought, but at least brief.

The next morning a beautiful lady, who I guessed to be in her late twenties, came to talk to me. She told me that she had rushed home to tell her father what I had said because she and her father had decided years before that she would only marry a man who would marry her without a dowry being paid. No suitor had as yet agreed to those terms so she was still single. When she told her father what I had said, all one sentence of it, they had started to laugh and they laughed and danced for hours. The unspoken shame they felt lifted. For me it was worth going just for that, although a lot more than that happened.

We spent a couple of days all together, and then scattered all over the country in two's and fours and sixes. Grace and I and Nancy, with her friend from Mexico, found ourselves in a town we had never heard of, had our meals delivered in plastic bags tied up with string, and did our best not to offend local culture. Grace and I slept on beds without sheets because, somehow the information of needing to take all sorts of things did not get to us, and fell in love with the ladies we encountered. We had this wonderful room where we looked out over the town watering hole and saw every sort of person, transport, and animal arrive there. It was a real view of small town life.

The meetings were held in a not yet completed cinema, without lights. It was the best venue that could be found. And worked just fine, for we all wanted to listen and to learn. There were so many needs, some spoken of, most not. I learned at a new level the power of silent empathy. And also how the simplest thing can work wonders. I still remember the compelling needs the women who came had, and their simple faith as they asked for God to come.

I remember one lady who looked as though life had been a struggle from day one. She asked for prayer for her arm. We didn't need to ask what was wrong as somehow her forearm was bent at right angles halfway between her wrist and elbow. We asked how it had happened. Her grandson had lost his temper with her and hit her with what sounded like a club, and this was the resultant damage. We asked why the hospital had not set it for her, and found that she had not been allowed to get medical help lest the grandson found himself in trouble. I would like to say that we prayed and it straightened, but that didn't happen. But, as we prayed she said it felt far more comfortable.

Every person wanted prayer, both at the meetings and wherever we were. Exhausting and heartbreaking.

Back in South Africa we continued out travels to different groups and places. We noted that the name John Wimber kept coming up and heard tales of a new church group in America called *The Vineyard*.

I thought nothing of it until two things happened on the same day: I got a letter from England with a cheque in it to pay for me to go to one of John Wimber's conferences in Los Angeles, and also a letter from a friend in Hong Kong suggesting in the clearest terms that I should try and get there. I had to face that all this constituted guidance to go.

Reluctantly I went, as flying was definitely not one of my favorite past times, and LA was as far away as one could get.

I got there, having flown over the North Pole and been awed by just how much snow and ice lay below the plane. Once I found where I was staying, I queued to get in to the venue.

There was a long line both ahead and behind. After a while, the lady in front of me turned to talk to me. She asked me where I was from, so I told her South Africa. Her immediate response woke me up with alarm. "Do you know Grace and Helen?" My answer was slower. "Well yes," I admitted. "How well?" I thought and said honestly, "As well as anyone I suppose."

She proceeded to tell me all the stories she had heard, and there seemed rather a lot. None of them were quite accurate, but all nearly. I didn't know what to do. I desperately wanted to remain anonymous, having heard how Americans love celebrities. I had never thought of myself as one and had no desire to fit the role, as shyness has been a lifelong struggle. Her enthusiasm kept up until we reached the front of the queue. As she turned to leave she asked me what my name was. "Isobel", I truthfully replied. (It really is, I am just never known by my first name.) So I managed to avoid fame and got on with concentrating on the conference, which was why I was there.

I was meandering back from the ladies during an interval when someone stopped me. "Why aren't you at the South African meeting?" they asked. I hadn't known there was one and found myself thrust into it, interrupting John mid sentence. "Who are you?" He asked. I was tempted to answer, "A voice crying in the wilderness, help!" but instantly thought better of it. I said I was from SA and had been told to come. "What do you do there?" John inquired. I replied that I spent a lot of time trying to help others. "How do you do that?" was his response. A hard one to answer briefly. I thought for a moment. "Well, I listen to them and I listen to God and I try and match the two …" I petered to a halt.

The result of that conversation was that he asked Grace and I to run the conferences he was planning to hold in South Africa the following year, which was 1988.

All our friends got involved. Thank God for such friends! People we didn't know got involved. Our dear friends from Soweto got involved. Everything that could go wrong did. It was exhausting, nightmarish and endlessly demanding. In the end it seemed to be worth it as so many were thankful for the benefits they found from attending.

Most of the helpers were relieved that we made the finishing line.

We still meet individuals who are grateful.

But for us perhaps the most moving and important thing of all was that afterwards three friends from Soweto invited Grace and I to a meal. Nic was one of our closest friends, and he, Jamieson and Vic had been involved from the beginning. They had been part of the growing Vineyard group of churches long before we had even heard of it. They had been watching with interest as we fielded disaster and discouragement and opposition, as such things seemed to be collecting as surely as dust accumulates.

They told us that they had been waiting for us to quit. Then they met and asked themselves why we didn't quit. They admitted to us that they would have done so given the difficulties and opposition.

Finally, they said they caught the reality that if one is asked by God to do something like this, quitting is not an option. They wanted to keep in contact with us even though the conference was over.

We became very good friends, and met regularly for years afterwards, for coffee or a simple meal, caught up with each other's news, and tried to find the next stage in the journey, particularly with Nic.

Grace and I became good friends with him and often met for coffee or a simple meal together, and just caught up on news and pondered a way forward. He was wonderful company. One day he said to us that he thought God had given him some words for us. Here are the words we have never forgotten. "Waves of discouragement will break over you, they will keep breaking over you. But I have lit a fire in you that will not go out." How very much we have needed to be reminded of them in the following years.

We thoroughly enjoyed the visits of Jackie Pullinger from Hong Kong. Her meetings were all 'let's practice what we are talking about' ones and such fun, as well as allowing a lot of people to change forever.

She impacted groups all over the country, particularly the younger generation, and we simply loved having her.

We visited her in Hong Kong too, and enjoyed being part of her wonderful outreach to drug addicts (her book *Chasing the Dragon* tells the story so well). It was also great being part of something we did not have to organize.

Since moving down to Franschhoek in the western Cape we have managed to keep the Conferences smaller. The first was called 'Outward and Inclusive', and brought us back to the basics of the good news. It's all about people and moving forward. I loved the simplicity and hope it offered of achieving change not just discussing it.

Then there were two led by Catherine Fabiano from the USA. A psychologist and pastor, she spoke on healing our pasts to release our futures, and many found the input refreshing, offering relevant ways of dealing with and being healed of 'old stuff.'

The last one we did was simply called 'The Gathering.' We invited anyone who wanted to come.

We were given the Sport's Centre in Groendal as the biggest space we could find that was the easiest to get to. The sessions were from 9–12 in the morning and 5–8 in the evenings, so anyone could make it at some point.

All we offered was music, and input from Jackie Pullinger on how to receive and use God's gifts. Of course there was ministry and people received gifts of different kinds for themselves.

If it sounds a bit chaotic, perhaps it was, but most of the folk who came loved it. It simply let everyone come and go as they wanted, and for many of us it was the most space we had been allowed for a long time. Perhaps ever, for many of those who attended had come from shack-land.

A LAST COMMENT ABOUT A CONFERENCE - THE ONLY TIME EVERYONE WAS HEALED

It was during desperate times in the nation. The struggle to overthrow the existing government was obviously going to be successful. But, as it grew closer, the battle intensified and the level of anger and violence increased.

At this unlikely time we were organizing a conference on healing. Unexpectedly we had been asked to do so, and had said yes.

It could not have been at a more difficult time, and it was turning out to be even more nightmarish than we had anticipated. Just as one thought "It cannot get worse," it did. We were working as hard as we could, travelling everywhere, and helping our team put together this big conference at Nasrec

Then, as though there was not enough to do, we got a call from a pastor in a city at the other end of the country. "Please come down. The comrades in the township have said no one can come to your healing conference. They don't believe any one will get help. And it has become a target for anger. But we have people who want to go. The comrades say they will burn down the homes of any who attend and attack the individuals. Please come and sort it out for us."

The threats were real and chilling. Our first thought was, "If the locals on the spot cannot sort it out, what on earth do they expect us to do?" A very fair conclusion we thought. But it gave us no peace, and they didn't either. So we got into the car and drove across the country to this city. We had no idea what we would find or what we could do.

The next day, a Saturday, we were driven through townships obviously in turmoil to our destination, which was in an area famous for the intensity of the struggle for freedom. The road was littered with the detritus of previous struggles, broken bottles, burnt rubbish, makeshift barricades.

On the way I saw a young man running from an angry crowd. They were throwing stones at him and he was shielding his head as best he could as he ran. As we watched in horror he was surrounded. I asked the driver to stop. He refused. I screamed at him and tried to get out, but the doors were kiddy locked. We turned the corner, and the last thing I saw was someone heaving a large brick at the doomed man. Grace and I felt sick and helpless and compromised. We arrived at the hall in no state or mood to talk about healing, or anything else.

The place had about fifty people in it, and the comrade. There was no doubt about who he was. With no introduction or greeting he pointed to where we were to sit, and then said, "Start." Grace bravely did, and spoke quietly and with conviction about the upcoming conference, and realistically about what we hoped for.

The comrade could not have made his anger more obvious. I found myself sympathetic. What possible relevance did a conference on healing in Johannesburg have for the people of this community?

Yet, healing at any level had to be worth having, particularly if God was in it. And there were people from the community who wanted to go.

The comrade's anger was about to explode over both of us, stupid white women who were making terrible things worse. His contempt for us could not have been plainer. It was hard to see how thing could get worse, but it did look as though that was the way we were going.

I interrupted Grace, in that desperation that enables one to do things that, later, leave one shattered. "You don't believe a word of this do you?" I said to the Comrade. "No" was the truthful reply. After all, why should he? I continued, "Right, give us your sick. If they are healed then you will let the people come to the conference. If they are not then you will do what you are planning."

We faced each other in a room where everyone seemed to have stopped breathing. Certainly I had.

Then he looked around the room and pointed with his chin at the sickest looking person he could find. "Her," he said.

The people either side of her half carried, half dragged her to the front where, fortunately, there was a chair. As she sat there, probably as scared as we were, we prayed "Lord, this is your gospel not ours, please heal this woman." We did not ask what was wrong with her. There seemed no point. But, she was healed. Instantly. And everyone could see it, as did the comrade.

A long silence followed. He looked around again and pointed with his chin at another person and said, "That one."

He too was brought to the front. We prayed the same thing and saw the same result. He pointed to another, and another, and another. Finally there was no one left whom the comrade thought needed healing. "Go," he said and we went, on shaking legs, trying to look calm and also keeping up with the pastor who had brought us.

None of us said anything as we got back to where our car

was, and set off home to Johannesburg. The pastor had nothing to say except, "Travel safely". We managed a "Goodbye".

It was a long, hard journey home and we were exhausted and shattered. The terrible reality of where the nation was engulfed us, and the face of that young man being stoned was imprinted on our brains.

We made it to the flat and crawled into our beds.

The next day the phone call came through.

The comrades had lifted their ban on people coming to this particular conference. More than that, they would encourage those who wanted to, to come, and would pay for those who could not afford the travel expenses.

Perhaps, the possibility of God's healing coming to them, in their desperation, came closer.

This was one of the few times I have seen everyone who was prayed for healed. That is, physically.

The trauma of the nation is very far from dealt with. As a godly friend of ours had said years before, and it still holds true today, "If we could heal our past we would have a transformed people and the possibility of a very good future together."

That hope in itself makes it worth keeping going.

THE LADY AT THE CATHEDRAL

I never knew her name.

We met at the Cathedral at a healing service, held one Sunday afternoon each month. We were given forty-five minutes to preach, have it interpreted into two other languages, and pray for all those who wanted us to. 'We' were anything from six to ten volunteers, always with our hearts in our boots as we considered the impossibility of it all, and 'they' were anything from fifty to two hundred individuals with heartbreaks and desperate needs. It was a new service, introduced into the list of regular services at the insistence of some of the congregation. I suspect everyone wondered how it would go, and if it would achieve anything.

We became quite good at short testimonies that at least gave us some faith or hope or courage. Then we prayed with whoever came up, one on one. Some of the requests needed the gift of interpretation. "I want my ears to grow" was a cry to hear God better. "The cat came" a plea for protection from witchcraft. "I am afraid" could mean almost anything. We learned to depend on the Holy Spirit to be our teacher and guide with every breath. Many requests were all too clear. Desperately sick people. Children on drugs. Sons joining gangs and in trouble with the police. Endlessly, no jobs, no home, no money. People with AIDS, or relatives dying of it, and all the fallout from that – of the loss of wage earners, and more and more orphans somehow to be cared for.

We used to go home exhausted and broken hearted, and got into the habit of having pancakes together to give ourselves time to unwind, and perhaps to help us with the overwhelming sadness we encountered every time. And square our shoulders, at least metaphorically, when next time came round.

One day a lady came. She was very tall, with a commanding presence, and there was something about her that touched me deeply. "My son, he is no good. I have no other family. I only have one son, and he is no good. Please pray for him." I did, but she stayed. "Please pray for him every day this week," she said with intensity. I said I would. And I did.

The next month she didn't come up for prayer, but found me after the service. "Did you pray for my son?" she asked me. I said that I had, and was so pleased that I had done so. My answer was not enough. "Did you pray on the Monday", she asked, and I said "Yes." "Did you pray on the Tuesday, did you pray on the Wednesday, the Thursday, the Friday, and the Saturday?" Each time I said I had. After a long silence she said, "On Sunday they killed him." I was stunned. She only had one son. Now she had no family, in a culture where family is everything.

"What happened?" I whispered. She told me. On the Sunday her son was walking through the township. He passed two old ladies selling bananas. Following him were a group of young boys. As they got up to the old ladies, they knocked them and their table to the ground, stole the money and the bananas, and went past him, laughing. Her son said, "You should not have done that!" to them, so they killed him.

It was, sadly, not that uncommon a story. We looked at each other for what seemed like forever. Finally I said to her "He died a brave man." She fell on me, and wept and wept. "Those are the first good words I ever heard said about my son," she said, turned away and walked out of the cathedral. I could wash my clothes, go to the physiotherapist for my aching back, but nothing took away the pain in my heart. All I could do was to continue to pray.

The next month she found me at the altar rail. We looked at each other for some seconds, I had no words to say, and she said nothing. Then she turned away. The next month she found me again. The pain in her eyes was as present as last time, and I could think of nothing to say as we shared her grief together. She again turned away. This went on month after month. She found me; the pain was the same, as was my silence. I could never think of anything at all that might help. I started to try and avoid her by moving along the rail or to the Lady Chapel. Every month she found me, and we shared the silent pain. I got to the stage where I wished I could go down with flu or malaria just to avoid these moments of unresolved fierce pain and my failure to offer anything.

It went on, for two whole years. Then she broke the silence. "I want you to know you have loved me better," she said. She hugged me, turned away, and I never saw her again.

I do not know what my silence meant to her, or my recognition of her pain that went beyond words. I do know that for two long years I had longed for God to give me some word or answer, or anything, to meet her need. I had no understanding at all of what God had been doing between us. I went home with a great burden lifted, and the certainty that God did not need my words, just my willingness to be there.

I will never forget her.

TWO BECOME THREE

I was at a church weekend lead by a great friend of mine who was the rector. The surroundings were beautiful for it was set in the Magliesberg, a lovely mountainous area north of Pretoria. All should have been well, but it wasn't. For Grace was in England, and I was left doing the scheduled speaking.

I had a lifelong difficulty in speaking to a group. At school I did not. When I went to College to train as a teacher of physical education, I had reckoned on needing to say very little. However, I found out how bad my problem was when, in groups of three, we were taken to schools to give lessons, one teaching and the other two watching, learning and commenting. The other two did fine. I could not get a word out. That could have been the end of it all, except the principle of the College took me in hand and painfully trained me on how to do it. I remained a very non-verbal teacher but gradually mastered the art of it all. Grace helped me enormously and we had an agreement, if I dried up, she stood up. But she was not there.

I was sitting on the grass, a reluctant speaker wishing I wasn't there, and I looked up and saw Jane with the same expression on her face I probably had on mine. We laughed, talked, and became friends. It made such a difference to the weekend, and has gone on doing so ever since.

Jane Bewsey quickly became part of all Grace and I did, and

we often spent time together. Grace and I ran courses, created jobs, visited townships, and all the rest we did, while Jane worked all hours at her medical practice. It was wonderful and proved the truth of the saying 'two is better than one but three is better still'. We loved the widening of our understanding and the sharing of the ups and downs together. Our lives became more and more entwined until one day Grace said, "This is silly, she lives in our suburb in a too large house and we in a flat, why don't we buy a house we can share." And being Grace, she went looking. One day she announced, "I have found it", and indeed she had. It was at a price we could just manage between us, had a house in the front that Jane could use and a lovely cottage at the back for us ... it even had a swimming pool. Perfect indeed.

The three of us began to have holidays together, and some of the happiest times we had were in Europe courtesy of timeshares Jane had invested in. We went to a snowbound Austria, due to an unseasonal snowfall when we had hoped to see the spring flowers; saw something of France; loved wandering through Italy; and visited good old England as well. Jane went to Hong Kong with us and loved it. She embraced whatever she was asked to do and we had a lot of fun along with the hard work. She joined us in everything we were doing, and it was wonderful. Quite simply, the two had become three.

ELECTION DAY

26th April 1994 – election day had finally come. South Africa had been struggling through the appalling trauma of the apartheid system for decades. Of course it would be overthrown at some point, but when and at what cost, and what would remain and what would have been destroyed in the process, were all unknowns.

The long journey that had brought us to this point was past. The tragedy of the Soweto uprising, the wars in the streets and the murder of Chris Hani, the release of Nelson Mandela, the endless strain of the negotiations towards the creation of a new constitution and the setting up of free and fair elections had all happened.

The talking, the round the clock praying, the tiny individual efforts, and the great big ones from others, were over. Now we simply had to get out there and vote. I think it was fair to say that we had lived on the edge of being engulfed by the past for so long that everyone was exhausted.

Grace, Jane and I, like so many, were determined to vote on that first day. Voting was to last four days, but we wanted to be right in there from the start. The reality that we could be injured or killed, if predictions of violence were true, did not matter to any of us as much as being part of the first free and fair election in this troubled land. No one knew what the day would bring. The world press had turned up in their thousands, and many felt they had come to film a bloodbath. Many ordinary people thought they might be right. Certainly no one predicted what actually happened.

We got up, had breakfast, squared our shoulders and stepped outside ready to cope with whatever happened. I don't think I have ever been so surprised at what did.

We stepped into a peace that seemed to cover everywhere, like a blanket of snow that was deeper than any of us was high. It was the most amazing and unexpected thing. I think there were few who expected the day to be without violence, the question had been how much there would be and whether it would prevent the elections being accepted as 'free and fair'. And here we were walking along in this stunning peace.

We arrived at the nearest poling station and queued for ages before we were told that we had come to the wrong place, so we then walked to the right one. It seemed as though the entire population was on the move and everyone was friendly. That was a first. We exchanged smiles and greetings as if we all were friends. We arrived at the right poling station, and joined another queue, even longer than the first.

I mean long, it took us seven hours to get into the poling station itself. As we inched forward, we heard the stories of many of our fellow citizens who were either next to us, or wandering up and down the line, for there was no question that day of anyone pushing in, or of losing their place if they moved away for a time. Some went off to get food or water, which was often shared by those nearby. Places were kept as folk disappeared for a while. The peace that had covered the land seemed also to have transformed its citizens for that golden day. Oh how I wish that it had lasted. But it did give us a sense of what could be.

Finally we made it. We cast our vote. We went back home.

We thanked God for the miracle, and we marvelled as the four days continued in that unanticipated peace.

The world press was stunned. The people of the country united in their acknowledgement of the miracle. Some time later there was a service where everyone packed a stadium to say "thank you". It was such a good event to go to.

WHAT CAN WE DO
TO MAKE IT BETTER

Of course, the problem in going into the townships was what for? It was quite definitely not helpful just to visit. There had to be a reason that would help at least some. As we thought and prayed about it, the obvious starting point was job creation. For then, as sadly to this day, the massive lack of employment, with all the inevitable results of poverty, depression, hopelessness, and anger, were absolutely obvious. What to do about it was not.

I spent a long time thinking and praying about it. After all, my father had been a very effective and respected businessman in London, and I must have picked up something in all those years. And if not, God had all the answers. We needed something that anyone could have a go at, whatever their education and qualifications or lack of them. Finally, we got it. We called it *Iflend*.

It was simple.

Find a group in your township who want to work. We offer the following:

- We would lend R300 to five individuals within the group, interest free, to be payed back at R50 per week, each week.

- When all the loans had been payed back we would then lend to the next group of five individuals.
- They must choose a leader to whom all decisions and problems would go through.
- They must think carefully about what skill applicants had that would turn into an income.

When the community were satisfied that they had five applicants that had a viable idea, and they trusted them to pay back R50 per month, we would lend the money. We would come back each month to work through the successes and problems, and then, as a group succeeded, we would lend to the next. Of course, we spent ages checking and discussing and debating and starting again …

For instance, we went through each idea thoroughly with each individual, and discussed that individual with the group. We would then ask the group a number of questions like:

- Would the group buy that product at that price, and why?
- Would they trust this person?

When Grace and I had gone through this until we thought it had it's best chance, we then had to find folk who wanted it. As it had only just become possible for white people to go into townships without a permit, and as we had absolutely no idea where to start, we asked God to sort it out and started to share the idea to anyone we could. I spoke to every teller at the shops I visited. "By the way, we are starting a job creation scheme for people in the townships … here is a contact number …" Grace spoke to every clergyman she met. One day I heard her say to someone on the phone, "Micro lending, no we don't do that," and I quickly said "Yes we do, it's called *Iflend* …"

The caller belonged to a wonderful group of clergymen who

were bringing hope and good news to a very battered community. They asked to meet with us and we spent a long time talking about *Iflend* and something of what we had been doing down the years. They then introduced us to Gertrude Moyana, a wonderful heroine of the struggle, who had recovered from a devastating asssination attempt by authorities. She was a member of a group called *Khulumani*, and had a passion for the young victims of the AIDS epidemic. She was key in all we did initially in the Vaal triangle, and outwards throughout the Transvaal.

Very quickly she understood what we wanted to do, as she also saw community strength and strong relationships as key. She introduced us to her friends and arranged that we would start in Sebokeng, her home community. It felt like coming home.

Within a very short time we had a group started, the first month we went back everyone paid back their R50.00, one woman paid all R300 and said she had also bought a fridge, and the news spread like wildfire. As did *Iflend*.

MORE THAN A
LENDING SCHEME

As we kept going to Sebokeng we began to know people better, and they us. It took a long time for trust to come, but, as we kept turning up when we said we would, as one group paid back and the next started, as we encouraged those who were trying to expand what they were doing, or needed to add or alter to make it work, our relationships deepened and historical divides lessened. We also spent hours listening to stories, taking part somewhat in the discussions, and above all singing and praying. We became a group.

From the beginning, as we talked together, it was all too obvious that healing was needed from the trauma and abuse so many had suffered, Also, from every imaginable illness – some we had never heard of. We prayed about the injuries and the abuse, the effects of the police and military swooping into the townships and tracking down marked people.

Gertrude was one such person. A marksman had shot her and she was the only survivor of the seven targeted by him that day. These were emotional times as hurt and stress and grief and anger were allowed to surface. We said almost nothing, joined in the praying, and left weeping. We didn't ask any questions, it was much too private for that.

Soon Gertrude took us to Evaton, a nearby township where

she also worked, and then Boipatong. And then into Soweto, into even further townships as the news of *Iflend* flew from place to place. I suppose the rarity of good news was the major factor. Nic, our pastor friend who lived on the East Rand, contacted us quite soon after we started, because he was told of it, and we spent a lunchtime discussing the venture.

Because the thing just grew, we found ourselves all over Gauteng, sometimes with Gertrude, and sometimes without. Increasingly, because of the power of word of mouth, the good news travelled far and wide.

THE CLINIC

After many months, Gertrude began to talk about the sick in the groups, and how difficult it was for them to get treatment. It was a long and emotional story and involved the problems of too many sick people, overloaded clinics and hospitals, the struggle for many in the groups to get themselves anywhere because of their injuries. We didn't see how we could help in this, but as we talked about it with Jane, and she had an idea.

At that time Jane was running her own medical practice in Johannesburg, and was always at full stretch. But, she decided she could take one morning off a month and see if she could help the situation. So we talked this through together, and then with Gertrude who was more than happy with the idea. We agreed to give it a go. Gertrude talked to all the individuals who might want to come. We did our best to find the best day and time of the week, and we had to decide what in the world to take with us, for it all had to be taken each month, and who knew what bandages or drugs or other things would be needed.

What we had to provide Jane with was a room, a bed and water. I wish I had a photo of what we started and then ended with. It was a room on the first floor of an organization Gertrude was involved with. They let us use it without cost. A bed was found, however, the legs were six inches high, so Jane had to kneel beside her patients to examine them. Not ideal. The water was downstairs and along the corridor. We carried an uncountable number of buckets up the steep stairs.

We set off before 06h00 each time. That enabled us to get there and set up by 08h00. And it gave us the longest possible time to see most folk before we had to leave to get back to the Jo'burg practice. Breakfast was coffee from a thermos and a sandwich, and lunch often what was left, as we headed back, trying to negotiate the unpredictable traffic.

So, we started. Debbie took blood pressure readings and did glucose testing. Jane spent a good part of her morning on her knees because the bed was so low.

The account of the injuries suffered and terrible effects on the individuals and families was comparatively easy to make some sense of. Medically, that is. Emotionally, none of us ever got used to the awfulness of the stories. But the graphic details, spoken as if it happened yesterday, brought the pain close to all of us.

Jane contacted local doctors and hospitals, provided untold amounts of drugs, and most importantly, new hope.

Grace and I provided tea, biscuits, conversation and prayer. These were some of the most demanding and rewarding times we have had.

When Jane finally got home from a very long day, we used to share and laugh and grieve and discuss, and try to understand so we could cope better the next time.

This went on until those who needed the service had been slotted into the local public medical services.

But one effort is worth telling.

A blind man used to come. His blindness was a result of tear gas. He was without any vision at all. We got to know him. He was well educated and surprisingly lacking in bitterness.

The three of us decided to do what we could. We talked

with St Dunstan's, found a residential course our friend could attend, and off he went. He came back transformed; having acquired skills he thought had gone forever.

The last time I saw him he was an effective councilor for his community, full of confidence and living a full and fulfilling life.

APPLIED ARABIAN NIGHTS

We were in a township known both for the violence of its past and for the protection racket run by one of its more famous citizens. It never felt safe being there. It wasn't. And this time more than ever. It seemed as though everyone was holding his or her breath waiting for something bad to happen.

Gertrude, who had introduced us to the township and who knew it very well, said quietly "I think we need to leave as soon as possible." (She had been told, surreptitiously, by one of the people who lived there that the person who ran the protection racket saw us as a threat, both for our presence in 'their' patch, and because we charged nothing for what we did.) I thought for a moment and then gave my car keys to our friend Shauna, and told her to take everyone with her and, as soon as I heard the car start, I would follow.

I needed a way to distract the group as our lot made their exit and prayed desperately for an idea.

Then I remembered the story of the Arabian nights, and how the hero, threatened with death, kept telling stories, so I launched into one. I have no memory what it was but I told it with as much action and passion as I could muster, turning to this one and then that as I did so, trying to defuse the atmosphere.

It seemed forever before the car started, and I could feel the tension reach explosion point. Finally I heard that most welcome sound and, still pouring out the story, began to move across the room towards the door.

I had just reached the door and the possibility of safety when I was stopped in my tracks. An overwhelming putrid smell had distracted me. It was terrible, and as I looked for its source I saw filthy rags covering the feet of a woman who had just come in through the door.

I forgot all about leaving. "What is wrong with your feet?" I asked. "They have gone rotten," she replied. "Verily they have" I thought and instinctively I prayed, more in longing than in faith, "Jesus, please heal her feet."

She let out an ear-shattering shriek and I left as fast as I could. I was surprised that no one followed, as there had been a growl of rage when I had reached the door that had unnerved me.

Gertrude was thrilled to see me and we headed for our homes in relief.

The next day Gertrude phoned and told me that the group wanted us to go back as soon as we could. "What for, to kill us?" was my unenthusiastic response. I hoped never to go back. "No", she said, "the lady's feet were healed instantly and they want you to go back to pray for them all".

It was so hard to do so. But we did. Each time was hard. Each time we did not want to go.

Each time people were healed, they knew God had been with them, and only He knows what was achieved.

COME TOGETHER

Iflend was taking more and more of our time. Fortunately
Shauna and Jos started to come with us, to help with the groups
and just to be there with us. We needed their company badly.
They came to the groups, which took at least a whole morning,
and they came to the clinic, which also took a whole morning.
Others also came, and we were so grateful for their presence,
for there were always so many who wanted our time. Grace
and I still travelled and did other things, but our focus more
and more was the townships. Particularly Sebokeng. This was
because of Gertrude.

She knew Sebokeng. She had been part of the struggle. She
had worked for years for an organization called *Khulumani*,
which existed to help victims of The Struggle. It was she who
took us to place after place. It was she who had the credibility
and was able to give us some. It was she who knew what was happening, and when to do what. She was our teacher in so many
things. And it was she who was responsible for the next move.

For Gertrude had started to talk about finding a home for
the orphans. Again and again, it was the inevitable subject every
time we met. Of course it was, as she was agonizingly aware of
the growing number of child headed families all around the
area. This was the era of the AIDS epidemic before medication
was available. Children, barely in their teens, were having to

care for their younger brothers and sisters because their parents had died and no one else was there to look after them. She was already trying to help what seemed an extraordinary number of them as well as all the groups she was involved with through *Khulumani,* and now *Iflend.* But where she lived offered no solution. She was renting a room no bigger than a garage from a young man who was her landlord, and who also lived there.

It became as clear to us all that it was a need that had to be met. Grace and I spent many hours over coffee at Southgate, a shopping centre somewhere between Johannesburg and Sebokeng, talking about her dream and what that would mean in real terms. It was quite clear that she knew what she wanted. That it was a big enough dream and also small enough that we could give it a go.

So we started to look for a house. We didn't have the money to buy it, but on the basis that it was right, and that we didn't need the money until we found somewhere, we started to look.

Well, to be honest, Grace and I saw the need, but it was Shauna, who had lived in the area, who went house hunting. Of course what we were looking for was a house in a safe area for her in the heart of Sebokeng. So Shauna and Gertrude drove to lots and lots of places, and looked at many different possibilities, but it was difficult to find a safe place. One house was between a brothel and a shabeen. Another was in an area too close to an all-men's housing facility, a notorious place for rapes and attacks. Still another was right on the freeway with no fences to keep the children safe. One was on the border of a dumpsite with many vagrants around. Finally Gertrude said that there was another place, but it was a little out of Sebokeng, and it was a farm. It was for sale.

So they went to see it. It had been a caravan park, and had a few buildings still standing, but was abandoned, and was being systematically dismantled brick by brick by needy neighbors. Also there was a dispute among the owners about whether they wanted to sell it and who would get the proceeds. Clearly this was not the place. Then the caretaker said, "But the farm next door but one is for sale too".

So they drove there. In Shauna's words:

We got out of the car on the dusty, dry, dirt road that went up to the barely standing gate, and saw a small notice that the owner had written on a board and tied to the gate stating that he wanted to sell and giving his phone number. The caretaker of the property came ambling up to us with a dog in tow and asked if he could help us. His T-shirt was torn in many places and his tattered shorts would have fallen off if not for the cord tied around his waist, and he was barefooted. He looked as derelict as the farm did. But he offered to show us around and confirmed that the owner wanted to sell and that he would be home later that day. I phoned the owner and asked if we could in fact take a walk around the farm with his caretaker. He was happy for us to get the tour.

Gertrude and I walked all around the outside of the various buildings accessing whether this could work or not. Gertrude was overwhelmed and anxious about the size of the grounds. She was used to a very crowded and noisy neighborhood with the neighbouring houses a meter or two away on all four sides, along with loud music, screaming children, arguing adults and noisy, barely road worthy cars.

This was a few kilometers out of town, and the nearest farms a few acres away on all sides. Birds were singing in the trees and the wind was whispering through the leaves. I saw the potential. I thought it was wonderful. Gertrude could only see the snags. But it was the best we had come up with after such a lot of searching.

So Shauna phoned me. "I am standing in a field on the road from the N1 highway to Sebokeng, and I think I have found the house we are looking for", she announced. "It is a farmhouse on a small farm and seems ideal."

It was. It was on the main road which gave easy access, quite close to the town of Sebokeng, reasonably accessible for schools, and surprisingly cheap. There were two houses, the main one, on the road was both big enough for Gertrude, her family and a number of children. The other one, about 100 yards away, was ideal for more orphans and a housemother. Then there was a third building which could be used either for job creation or as a school, and numerous sheds. Also about 10 hectares of land, an orchard, a Dutch barn ideal for kids to play in, and a nice garden in the middle of the buildings, ideal for gatherings.

We somehow found the money, started an organization, which we called *Come Together*, and bought the farm.

I shall not forget the day we moved in. Gertrude looked terrified, she was shaking so much that the farmer's wife found a blanket to wrap her in. She and her husband could not have been nicer, and they left everything they did not want to take, so the house at least had some furniture. Gertrude brought all she had and we found the rest as best we could.

It was wonderful and awful. We now owned the farmhouse, another house a hundred yards away, some sheds and outhouses and 10 hectares of land. And an orchard of sorts.

We cried out for volunteers to come and help, for we were so out of our depth that we didn't even bother reaching for somewhere we could put our feet on. The whole thing was far bigger, and needed more doing to it than we had contemplated in our wildest dreams, and yet put right, offered all that could make the dreams come true.

But help we needed. Badly. Fortunately we got it. Denham

and Jenny, from our previous church in Dorset caught the vision, raised money, and came to help. They were wonderful, refreshing, encouraging, and importantly, hands on.

Then Jackie Pullinger sent a team to help. They painted and cleared and altered and mended. They went around singing and lightening the place up. We locals went as often as we could, partly to help, but also to enjoy their company. We also took an enormous amount of rice and noodles and other food that met the Chinese visitors' preferences.

My memories get blurred when I think of this time because so much was happening. The house was adapted to provide for Gertrude, her immediate family, and her extended one. She moved in with her daughter, Nonky, and a friend. With great difficulty we adopted dogs from the local SPCA. They were great for security as well as companionship. We put up security lights and fixed the gate.

We went as fast as we could, and our volunteers as well, for whatever our needs and problems, they were insignificant compared to those of the orphaned children around us.

Slowly things started to improve. We didn't wait until everything was ready, but started to fill up with children. Gertrude was more than familiar with children who were desperate, and we soon found them on the farm. Within no time at all we had five children, four boys and a girl, Lorato, staying at the farm. Of course there was enough red tape to get strangled in, but with help from the widest assortment of individuals who seemed to turn up when we were stuck, we managed to get the necessary permission for Gertrude to care for them. One of the boys had been born HIV positive, but had not been diagnosed with it or had any treatment. Jane picked up that that might be the cause of his ill health, and finally managed to get him tested. The delay was because the rules said no child could be tested without the consent of the parent or guardian. That poses a problem when there are neither, and shows so clearly the nightmare we were all living in.

Each child came in with a story, and each one was heart breaking. One child had been repeatedly beaten and raped. Her head and shoulders were covered with open wounds where she had been frequently beaten with sticks and belts. Another had been looked after by a brother who had just dropped out of school. Soon afterwards he was killed in a car accident. Grandparents were looking after a young boy. Except they were not. They were both alcoholics and interested only in themselves, using the grant to care for their grandson to provide alcohol for their parties. The list was endless, and we quickly had to face that we could only do what we could.

Gertrude's friends soon got involved and would chat and clean and cook and sit either at the old farm table or under the huge old pepper tree just outside with the children sharing mealtimes. They offered a real and tangible sense of family and belonging.

We found schools, coped with the shopping, bought Gertrude a car, and attempted to start a vegetable garden. It was all go all the time.

Jean, a cousin of Jane's, helped us with the legal side, and her firm began to support us financially as well as occasionally sending teams to help us with a specific project – of which there was an endless list. Over time we got rid of the junk that filled so many rooms, sheds and unlikely places, and created useable spaces for the children to play and learn. We had a crèche, we provided food, we had a sewing group, and the endless job of adapting, repairing and developing what we had. We ended up with classrooms, a large play space, play equipment, slides and swings in the garden.

And we had the land. Acres of it. Debbie tried everything that she knew, everything that she could find out, and put a huge amount of work into trying to get a sustainable vegetable garden going. Everyone agreed it was a great idea. No one else stuck it out. The men who were interested wanted to own the land, not just have their own area. I think the work she put in at least equaled the effort she made to walk up to base camp on Mount Everest, and was at least as attainable. As we could get no buy-in from the local men we turned a large part of it into a football field.

Jos ran cooking classes and also did classes with the children. She also offered to help train the preschool teachers.

We built waterless loos when that technology was in its infancy. We pruned the fruit trees. We tried everything we could to get *Come Together* working for the children who came to live there, for those who came to the crèche, for those who came in the holidays, for those who came for parties. So many came to help, to give and to be part of it.

The camps in the school holidays became a big thing. Gertrude would fill the farm up with kids who would have been on their own at home, and gave them a taste of belonging and being carefree.

We used the space outside the main house as a childrens play area, with sand, water, balls, food, drinks and fun! We tried everything we could think of to give them a good time. And somehow it worked, and there were enough helpers, food and goodwill to make it a success.

Chris West-Russell had been making CD's for us since the early days, so we began to scatter those to the interested. Cliffe Dekker became involved in a big way and provided the backbone of support.

When we were leaving to relocate to the Western Cape,

Leonia, Chris's wife, took over the running of the organization *Come Together*. She and her friends, who wanted to do something to make life better for those less fortunate than themselves, have been the ones who developed the project into something wonderful.

Gertrude is still the heart at the center of it all.

THE LUNCH THAT
COST A HOUSE 2006

We – Helen, Grace and Jane – were in Cape Town for a few days. Partly it was a break from a hectic time in Johannesburg, and partly we were looking at the possibility of selling the two flats Grace and I owned in Cape Town.

They were beautifully situated opposite the lighthouse in Milnerton, and we loved them. But, they were in an old block, and they effectively constituted our pension. We arranged to see the agent on the following Friday. We asked Grace what she would like to do on Thursday, which was her birthday. "I would like to have lunch at *Le Petite Ferme*" she said.

"Where is that?" we asked.

Having elicited that it was in Franschhoek, an area none of us knew at all, we set off.

Franschhoek is in an enchanting valley, surrounded by beautiful mountains, and is a charming, slightly old world village, with one main street and no traffic lights. We loved it.

For a couple of years we had found ourselves wondering where we might retire to when our jobs in Jo'berg were over, so we decided we would look at the retirement home in the village. It took me ten seconds to realize that it was not what we were looking for. We headed instead for a walk down the street.

There were some wonderful shops and lots of estate agents.

We found ourselves laughing at the prices, which were way beyond anything we could consider.

Then we saw one that was much lower. "Goodness," one of us remarked, "One that we could afford!" The agent stepped out of the door and said he would take us to see it. Sweeping aside our protests that we were not looking for houses, he bundled us into his car and drove us to a wine estate we had passed on our way in. It seemed fun, if slightly absurd, to be there, but he stopped outside a smallish corner house, announced that this was it, and we all clambered out. Grace went in first, said "I could live here!" Jane followed her, and repeated her statement, so I went in thinking "Well, I will have to". But as soon as I saw it, I agreed with them.

It seemed to have been designed with us in mind. Small enough for us to cope with, three equally sized bedrooms, and a view to die for. We loved it, expressed our pleasure, and went to lunch.

We celebrated Grace's birthday, had a great meal and I said over coffee that I thought we should put in an offer. The others inhaled their coffee in astonishment. But we had nothing to lose if we did, and everything if we did not, so we went back to the agent. He took our offer, told us that the house price had been dropped by R200,000 the day before for a quick sale. We left in a daze.

The next day our agent came to the Milnerton flats. In case we might want to sell he had already worked out what he thought we might get, exactly one third of the price of the Franschhoek house each, and said he had a potential buyer for Grace's and saw no difficulty in the sale of mine.

To continue the almost fairy story, Grace had a cash offer the next day, mine sold in a week, and Jane raised her share.

After two years of a tenant living there while Grace and I finished our work in the townships and Jane wound up her medical practice, we moved from Johannesburg to Franschhoek.

It remains a dream house and we still revel in the wonder of it all.

MOVING SOUTH

The three of us moved down to Franschhoek in 2009. Candidly, we wondered what we were coming to.

Jane had closed her medical practice.

We had resigned from the board of the old age home we had been part of for ages – Jane as their doctor, Helen as the Chairman of the Board, and Grace as the one who oversaw the building of the Alzheimer's Centre, and multiple other things. That constituted a pretty comprehensive departure from more than Johannesburg.

We said a heart-wrenching goodbye to Gertrude, the people in the lending schemes, the townships, and particularly *Come Together* and all the children there. That Jos and Debbie and Jean and Shauna were still there meant the gap we left was not too big, but it was hard for us.

Chris, who had done the initial videos of *Iflend* and the subsequent ones of *Come Together* continued to be a major supporter of it all, and his wife Leonia took over the chairmanship of the *Come Together* company. So many friends we had to say goodbye to.

Then there was all the turmoil of moving. We started to do the vast number of things it takes. We knew we were moving into somewhere much smaller so downsized radically. It was hard to let go of treasured things. (It helped if they were obviously too big.) Two of us went down to the house and took photos of the rooms. The three of us drew a scale plan, and really did take only what would fit in. I do regret some of the things I left behind, particularly my slides of our trip to Afghanistan, but moving is not easily achieved without error, and irrational decisions at times. We chose a moving company, (and definitely got that one wrong), set a date, and were ready to leave as soon as everything was packed on to the mover's truck.

It was a great journey, and we took it fairly gently, and with great joy drove along that beautiful road from Paarl to Franschhoek absorbing the awesome beauty of the valley. It was a moment of wonder when we unloaded the cars, put on the kettle we had brought with us, and absorbed our wonderful mountain view. There wasn't a lot more we could do except blow up our air mattresses, eat a brief meal and crash out. Very simple really as our small cars only had space for a kettle, our blow up mattresses, a picnic basket and a small selection of clothes.

The next day we found that our mover was charging almost double what we had agreed on and would not deliver until we paid his additional charge. Even when we paid we had days to wait. The van had not even left Gauteng.

A sad last memory of our time in the North, but nothing could quench the wonder we felt as we began to explore the village. It was the place of dreams. Big enough to have all we needed, small enough to have a hope of getting to know people easily, full of interesting and friendly people, and we hadn't heard a single gunshot after a week ... In the North we heard them every night.

We went to a church on the first Sunday and were immediately welcomed into the group. Here we met many of our friends that we still have today. We walked into the township without any fear and were greeted by a number of individuals. One lady, seeing us wander past, came out of her house, asked where we were wanting to get to, and proceeded to walk around with us. Really it could not have been easier or more generous. Jane worked part time for a local GP, but soon realised that the medical part of her life was over, and so became free to do what ever came up. And lots did.

Then we met Ron. A retired airline pilot who was running something called FRANCO, a nonprofit organization that seemed to try to meet all the emergency needs of the valley, and particularly in the township. Already people were pouring in from the North, and shack land grew as one watched. There was a huge need to offer help when there was heavy rain or strong winds or, the ultimate terror, shack fires.

We found out how large the heart of many were after the first, quite big, fire we witnessed. The smoke and flames and confusion were obvious from our home. (Our house is close to the township, just a couple of roads away.) We had been told what to do by Ron, so we loaded our car with essentials, food, blankets, toothbrushes, whatever we had spare, and headed for the church that was the collection place. As we drove up we saw a number of cars driving down that had obviously beaten us to it. And, as we drove back home we passed a whole lot more going up. It was so very good to see the response and be able to be part of it.

Of course we tried to get involved in everything we could. The result has been that we have. From volunteering at the Parkrun to being involved with the community organizations in the town. Jane is now on the board of FRANCO and in-volved in all sorts of things from sorting out a website with help from her son who is an IT expert, to buying gardening tools for the disabled group.

This group was something we got involved in quite soon after getting into the valley. We encountered Jim, Abraham and James. They had a largish plot just outside town, and it was full of excellent vegetables. We helped them with equipment and transport, and they started to sell their produce at the market

Then, without warning, the plot was sold and they had to leave. They were not even given time to move all their stuff somewhere else. It was heartbreaking.

Now Jim, the green fingered leader, has taken over most of our garden and is growing vegetables for our benefit and to take any extra into the townships to give to those who need it. He also gives young plants to those who will grow them and turns their tiny gardens into productive ones.

Of course the dream, shared by the local councilor, is to have a garden-township. Which, looking at the lovely gardens that are already there, is not impossible.

We've done lots of one-off help for individuals, folded pancakes at festivals, helped crèches to get going. In the process we have got to know folk from all over the valley and feel part of it. As a reward we have more friends than we dreamed of.

Then there was the market. We had not been here very long when Jane was asked to take it over. It was quite small, not thriving, and met on a Saturday morning under the oak trees in the church grounds. The person who had been running it could not any longer and decided we were just the people he needed to hand it over to … It was quite nerve wracking at first, and a very steep learning curve as we stumbled along. But everyone was friendly, and at least the stallholders knew what they were doing. It was great to become part of it.

One of the problems we hit was the lack of a cheese table. So we went to find a local supplier. We got to know the lady in charge of a company, not too far away, and bought from her.

This met the need and we asked her the answers to the questions the customers endlessly asked us.

This led to quite a lot of coffees with her, and it became clear that she was looking to start her own cheese company, without all the vastness and commercial pressure attached to the large concern she was involved in. We got talking with her about what she would need. A small place, was her answer, perhaps just a couple of containers, and an adequate electricity supply. We talked about it many times, as this was obviously her dream. As we had spent years in the North helping ordinary folk with far less knowledge than she had, we could see no reason why we could not look to see if her dream could realistically be realized.

So we spoke to a friend who knew about such things – I suspect him of knowing just about everything to do with farming – and we started a small venture on a small piece of land in Paarl. It cost a lot more than she had calculated, and there seemed enough red tape to stretch around the globe and then some spare, but finally we got it up and running. She brought most of the equipment we needed with her, and we provided the rest.

In the beginning it seemed to go well. She made good cheese, and we found enough customers. We were not making money, but there was every reason to push forward. It seemed as though her dream was being realized. In the process, of course, we learned more and more about cheese and cheese making, visited endless cheese making companies and went to see what those who sold it were selling. It was a lot of work, a whole new subject to try and get on top of, and we learned fast. We also did all the deliveries, and got to know customers for miles around.

Then the problem emerged. She could not consistently make good cheese. I suspect she simply lacked something inside her that would enable her to do so. Her lapses and short cut habits began to affect the consistent quality of her product. We dealt with all the equipment needs. Finally, at her request, we employed the man who had been her number two. He had been watching our venture, and was more than keen to be part of it. That seemed to stabilize things and they were better for a while. But we knew we lacked knowledge about cheese making. We had only volunteered to get the project up and running, and then they could buy it from us at cost as it became viable.

But unfortunately we had not solved the problem, as production was still not consistent. So we contacted the recognized cheese making expert and asked him to come and offer solutions. He was like an angel in disguise, absolutely on top of the subject, and full of simple and doable solutions. At the same time he was incredibly positive.

After one of his visits, the cheese maker left without warning because of his comments on many of the large cheeses maturing on the shelves. She thought they were maturing, he saw they were rotting. We had to throw them all away, so most of our stock was lost. This was really a sad ending to her dream. We never saw her again.

We spent a lot of time with the remaining cheese maker. We went through the whole situation from every angle, and so did our friend the expert. He had the ability, and he desperately wanted things to work. It seemed that he would succeed. Then the same failures appeared. It was unavoidably clear that he had learned all too well from his colleague how to take shortcuts, and was no more willing than she had been to change to doing it properly. So we closed the company.

What did we lose? Quite a lot of money, but not more than the limit we had set before we started the venture. What we gained was a whole lot of friends, the fun and interaction of running a stall at the market for some years, really feeling part of the valley, and the assurance that we had done all we could to make it work.

We then had time to get involved in other things. I'm now on the ACVV board. That is the Afrikaans Women's Christian Association. And I am the first English speaker thus honored. It is a real challenge to my minimal language skills, and I love it. ACVV is involved mainly in the care of women and children, and does fantastic stuff. They have been going since the Boer War over a hundred years ago, and are known for their consistent care.

Jane is heavily involved with FRANCO, a local orginisation. They have just moved office and are now in a little apartment on top of the ACVV offices in the township. The latest project is the clearing of the river that runs through Groendal and gets increasingly polluted and full of rubbish in the process. The instigator is Johnnie, an ex offender who delights us all with his sunshine approach to life and his deep commitment to Jesus. He is starting at the bottom. We are told another group is planning to start at the top, so there is a real chance of the river becoming very much better than it is at present.

There are many more projects we are involved in, from education to feeding the hungry, and caring for the desperate.

CLEANING THE STREAM

It started quite by accident really. Jane, who is involved with a local organization that tries to meet needs in the community, went to a meeting about the terrible state of the stream that runs through the township on the west end of Franschhoek. The stream emerges from the mountains next to a large primary school nestled just bellow the steep mountain, and runs more or less straight down the hill, under the main road, and then joins the Franschhoek river on its way to the sea. This slight valley is perhaps the most beautiful part of the town, with magnificent views.

They were worried about the alien vegetation which blocks the river flow, and contaminates as yet pure areas. After all the Cape Fynbos area is one of the seven Floral Kingdoms in the world and by far the smallest, and a wonderful treasure that needs to be guarded. So the group met and decided something needed to be done. But the issue of finance had yet to be resolved, and as always there was a lot of red tape to be sorted so nothing was being done.

Jane came back more worried about the endless heaps of rubbish. Scattered over the grass areas that run all the way down each side, as well as blown or thrown into the stream

Not just endless sweet and food papers and packets, but also bags of rubbish, and a lot of discarded furniture from houses and shacks on either side of the stream. Matresses, chairs, bed-frames and broken buckets, discarded clothes, tins and just about everything else imaginable, including dead animals. It seemed to Jane that it wasn't right for the people who lived there to have to live with all this, and we should look at what we could do to help.

Living at the top are so many people, and at night they, par-ticularly the women, do not feel safe going to the public toilets. Although there is a real attempt by the municipality to provide rubbish bins there are never enough. They get stolen, cut up and used for other things, or ignored as it is easier to dump stuff in the river.

On the other side of the stream, at the top where we started, is a single house standing on its own in a lovely little widening along the mountain. A large, brown dwelling with no visible windows and a huge green lawn, in spite of the drought. We are told that it is known as Sun City, and is very dangerous, for it is a stronghold of the drug lords, and they rule the river. All down the side of the stream, clusters of drug addicts collect for their next fix. It seems there is no attempt to avoid being seen, it is all quite brazen, and one can see who the suppliers are by the way the ordinary people step out of their way. We are told they are not pleased that we are happily making things better in the middle of their territory. But many of the residents are.

The upshot is that we now have a work force of ten people working four hours a day, Monday, Wednesday and Friday. FRANCO donates money that has enabled us to buy tools, gloves, wellington boots and masks (much needed in places). At the same time a man who runs a restaurant and deli in town asked Jane if she knew anyone who needed yesterdays bread. So all workers get a large loaf of bread. We have added soup in winter and hot chocolate in the mornings.

It still looks like a war zone, but the change is huge. Vast numbers of black bags have been filled. The local authorities are organizing different departments to remove the heaps of bags, and the large waste items like beds etc, and we have spoken to everyone who has asked us what we are doing, pointing out what a wonderful tourist destination it could be if it were clean, and how many jobs could be created when that happens.

It is tough, dirty, often discouraging and hard to bring hope back to a place that has lost it. But there are definite glimmers of hope – one being a meeting with the mayor that has resulted in more focus and help with the clean-up.

Does it look better. Most definitely. The river now flows rather than banking up against the litter, it is wonderfully cleaner although still not safe, the residents living on the banks either side often come and chat, and express their approval of the change. The area seems tangibly friendlier and old barriers are breaking down all the time. The drug lords still don't like us around as they hide their drugs in the vegetation in the river as the dogs cannot smell them there, and they fear that when it is clear they will not be able to do this any more.

It seems that one of the great benefits has been a change for the better for many. In attitudes, in relationships, in acceptance of others and in noticing what others are doing.

AND NEXT

In recent years, Grace's age began to catch up with her and we all tried to adapt to that. It has been hard for all three of us, as she moved into a retirement home in the village, and recently, decided she wanted to go back to England to be with her family in Gloucestershire. She left for England in August 2018.

Of course there is no ending to all this, for it is a way of life, not a project. We will simply continue to do what we can, to help those we can.

Some of it is predictable. Some just happens.

After all, we follow One who fed the hungry, healed the sick, and promised abundant life ... we can attest to that!

Printed in Great Britain
by Amazon

42813402R10099